TRAVELS WITH MY FRIENDS

Riding the train tracks to China

Nina Olsson

Grosvenor House
Publishing Limited

All rights reserved
Copyright © Nina Olsson, 2018

The right of Nina Olsson to be identified as the author of this
work has been asserted in accordance with Section 78
of the Copyright, Designs and Patents Act 1988

The book cover is copyright to Nina Olsson

This book is published by
Grosvenor House Publishing Ltd
Link House
140 The Broadway, Tolworth, Surrey, KT6 7HT.
www.grosvenorhousepublishing.co.uk

This book is sold subject to the conditions that it shall not, by way of
trade or otherwise, be lent, resold, hired out or otherwise circulated
without the author's or publisher's prior consent in any form of binding or
cover other than that in which it is published and
without a similar condition including this condition being imposed
on the subsequent purchaser.

A CIP record for this book
is available from the British Library

ISBN 978-1-78623-506-0

This book is dedicated to Simon and Penny who never once said to me, in any of my adventures, "What do you want to do that for?" but rather said "You go for it".

And 'Go for it' I did.

PREFACE

This book is taken from my diaries, reminiscences and the many photographs made during my 'trip of a life time', in the spring/summer of 2014. I retired from work that year and had decided to mark the occasion with something special. This was, of course, after consultation with my family, where the general consensus of opinion was "go for it", and so go for it, I did.

I had worked an extra five years (albeit part-time during this period) to supplement my pension and to give me the funding required. My immediate family were very understanding and I had their full support; in fact, my younger son and his wife came with me on the first leg of my journey.

My background, way back, is Swedish on my father's side, and French Romany way, way, back on my mother's side, although I and many generations have been born in England. I tell you this because I think it accounts for my need and want for travel, which I have done throughout my life.

After a fairly tame and settled teenage period, I decided at 18 to join the Territorial Army (T.A), which opened up lots of opportunities for me. I was able to do this and still work, which I had done from the age of 16. I loved it, and learnt amongst other things to drive a variety of vehicles such as five ton trucks, an Austin Champ jeep, and other skills associated with the military. I think this gave me my first taste for adventure, not on the climbing Everest type scale, but in a smaller, lower key way.

Through this, I met my husband, who was in the army, and with our two children travelled to different postings abroad, including a three year stint in Brunei, on the island once known as Borneo, now divided into part of Malaysia and Indonesian Kalimantan. An amazing experience, with miles of beaches, endless BBQs, jungle scenery, just a completely different way of life. I count myself very lucky for these experiences.

Following my later return to single life, I decided that I needed a higher paying job, so applied to university and did my degree in my 40s, a very mature student compared to my fellow classmates. I didn't need to worry; they were great, and we had a good three years with lots of hard work but also lots of fun. This then gave me the qualifications for my subsequent job at which I worked for over 20 years, which brings me back to the pension business and my 'trip of a lifetime'.

I had also done some other 'projects', like trekking in Nepal at 55 years old, and a Husky Sled Charity Challenge in the Arctic Circle at 61, so my family were not in the least surprised that I wanted to do something on my retirement.

Enough of the background stuff: I owe many people lots of thanks. Firstly my family, including sisters, Christine and Jean, and Mum for all of their support, including extra injections of cash from birthdays and Christmas. This trip was by no means cheap, but actually I never added up the total cost, just paid for what I could as I went along, and decided to worry about any debts when I got back.

Also to my friends, the ones who used their holidays to come and join me. You will be introduced to them individually in the course of the journey, as well as the ones who stayed at home, who were helpful, supportive and interested in what was going on. Tim, my grandchildren, and great grandchildren to whom I am just (crazy) Grandma Nina.

My thanks to those who have helped me with this manuscript: Carl for getting me the Laptop, David and Linda for proof reading, Paula for taking care of my cat Cairo Lancy, Lez and Ruby for talks on technical matters, Adrienne, Ann and other friends and family for their advice on various subjects. Also to 'Photo Corner Ltd', for printing all of my photographs. To Simon and Penny for their help and support in everything.

Speaking of photographs, if I have incorrectly identified a place, statue or artefact, please forgive me; they are right, to the best of my memory. Starting off with over 2000 images it has been difficult to know what to choose. Also I can't help the quality of the photographs taken through dirty train windows, but to my mind it just adds more atmosphere.

Some research was done using various sources, including 'Wikipedia', other Internet Sites, the Tourist Boards of various Towns/Cities, books, atlases, train and boat timetables and information from the diaries of my travelling companions. Also many hours of reminiscences and conversations with all involved.

Thank you also to Tamsin and all staff at Grosvenor House Publishing Limited for their help, advice and encouragement.

TRAVELS WITH MY FRIENDS

"All experience is an arch where through gleams the untravelled world, whose margin ever fades…….." ~ *Alfred Lord Tennyson*

Introduction

"You are going to be so bored now that you are retiring from work. What will you do with yourself?"

What will I do with myself? A question I fleetingly asked. "Oh, you mean after I have sorted out the house, done the garden, visited my friends, had experiences that only usually take place mid-week, and planned for my trip (a present to myself), and of course any on-going projects that I intend to immerse myself in. You mean that sort of bored?"

So, what of my present? I decided to plan a road trip, well rail trip really, to China. Yes, China. It had to be overland, so where to start: with an atlas of course. As this was to be an old fashioned trip, it had to be planned the old fashioned way, although I am not averse to using the odd bit of technology when needed. Actually the aids, in the form of my phone and tablet were used on a number of occasions; quite an achievement for a technophobe like me.

So, for a year I planned my way, paying for what I could as I went along. Being of limited funds I had to plan carefully. Don't we all. The trip was to last almost three months. The route was to say the least convoluted. Leaving my Birkenhead home, the first stop was London, then on the

Eurostar to Belgium. From there to Germany, up to Scandinavia, onto Poland, Russia, Mongolia and China, and that was just the outward section. Coming back, again via Russia, then Romania, Hungary, Austria, Czech Republic, Germany, London and home.

Must say it looked very easy on paper.

I mentioned my plans to my son Simon and to various friends. I said in passing that if anyone would like to join me, please do so. To my amazement twelve people said they would like to and proceeded to choose a meeting up point. Each person flew to a start point and in most cases, travelled by rail, with me to the next country. Also only the ones who travelled together saw each other, as it was mostly a case of one in, one out. What amazing bunch of people I know. How lucky am I.

The Planning

Firstly there were the visas to contend with, as the route went over Russian, Mongolian and Chinese territories. These could not be applied for too long in advance, so other sections of the trip were sorted first, with the hope that there would not be any problems with the visas. I was in touch with a company called Real Russia who did all of the arrangements for the visa applications and any other information that I required. The Staff were very helpful and friendly and felt like old friends at the end of it all.

I, in the meanwhile applied for any train tickets that I could buy in advance, the first being my Europe Rail Rover ticket. I felt like a student on a gap year, but I was a student retiree and my gap year was for the rest of my life, such fun.

Other tickets that needed advance booking were the overnight sleeper trains. Besides the trains, there was the accommodation to set up. I managed to book two flats, one in Moscow and one in Warsaw, also one small house in Beijing. The rest were diverse B&Bs, small hotels and even a couple of 5* abodes. All very different and all with their own merits, even including a cabin on a boat hotel in Stockholm.

Each was discussed with the particular friend who was joining me and occasionally booked by them. I also left most of the itinerary to them except for a few must-do things of my own. I felt that when people were giving all that time and effort, they needed to feel very much part of the whole adventure and not just tagging along with me. It was to be very much a participation sport.

As the start date got nearer I was able to book specific train tickets and had all accommodation verified. I also ordered my Currency for the different countries, such as Krona, both Danish and Swedish, Polish Zlotys, Russian Roubles and Chinese Yuan. I wanted to have some readily available cash for taxis and food on arrival at each location. I made up a paper file of all the pertinent paperwork to take with me and a copy of everything to leave with my son. Everyone was given an itinerary, including people at home like my Mum, sisters Christine and Jean and friend Paula who was kindly looking after my cat Cairo Lancy and my house. I'm honoured to know so many caring people.

The arrangements for the visas took some working out, particularly as the application forms were so thorough and complex. I had the photographs done and then sent the whole bundle of documents, including my passport, to the London Real Russia office. They then dealt with everything, thank goodness. They submitted the documents to all of the relevant embassies. One large nightmare sorted out for me.

Things of course are never straightforward so I was glad I had given enough time to allow for any hitches. I was impressed at how quickly the accommodation sites had responded, so that I knew at all times when and where I was staying at every step.

So, armed with all of the information gathered those last few months, the time to pack came very quickly. I don't know about you, but I am hopeless at choosing what to take, and in what quantity. The added complication was what to pack for the different regions being visited; snow in Sweden, rain in Europe and sweltering heat in China.

Consequently I ended up with far too much luggage; one case, one large bag, one rucksack, handbag, camera bag, oh and even the odd plastic bag. At least there were no luggage restrictions on trains. So here was where my planning fell down; any self-respecting backpacker would have had that all sorted easily. Christine came to help me and we managed to off-load some of it, but I still went with far too much. Fortunately for me, each friend took something home for me when they left.

My end plan was to have a get-together at my home on my return. My words to each of my travel companions on leaving were "see you in Denmark, Russia, China or wherever", and on their leaving me "see you in Rock Ferry". It sounded good.

So, what about Rock Ferry, the location of my home? It is a district of Birkenhead, part of the Wirral Peninsula on the banks of the river Mersey. Benedictine monks began operating the first ferry across the river to Liverpool as early as 1150, and the town was granted a Royal Charter by Edward 111 in 1330. An area of mixed fortunes, but prosperous during its shipbuilding heyday.

The Wirral is a place of beautiful vistas. There are beaches, green belt, the first ever public park on which New York Central Park is based, industrial areas and two rivers, the Dee and the Mersey. No matter where I have been, I have always loved to come home, but that would be for much later; many adventures awaiting first.

So, it was time to go. The transport was waiting, ready to take me off for the start of my

TRAVELS WITH MY FRIENDS

CONTENTS

Dedication... iii

Preface v

Introduction: Planning, Decisions, Timetables... ix

Chapter 1: Simon and Penny in Antwerp, Belgium, Alone in
              Cologne, Germany... 1

Chapter 2: Gill in Copenhagen, Denmark, and Gothenburg,
              Kiruna, Karlstad, and Malmo, Sweden 19

Chapter 3: Sandra and Helen in Warsaw Poland 47

Chapter 4: Collette and Kate in St. Petersburg and Moscow, Russia 61

Chapter 5: Jo in Moscow, Russia 83

Chapter 6: Trans-Siberian Train and Mongolia 97

Chapter 7: Jo in Beijing, China.. 129

Chapter 8: Alone in Beijing 149

Chapter 9: Vicky in Beijing, China 153

Chapter 10: Beijing experiences: Getting ready to move on................. 163

Chapter 11: Trip to the Yellow Mountains/Vicky 167

Chapter 12: Return to Moscow/Trans-Siberian Train/Vicky 179

Chapter 13: Vicky in Moscow, Russia 191

Chapter 14: Bucharest, Brasov and Sighisaora, Romania
with Vicky 205

Chapter 15: Gina in Budapest, Hungary and Vienna, Austria 241

Chapter 16: Liz in Prague, Czech Republic and Cologne,
Germany 261

Chapter 17: Linda in London, U.K. And HOME 285

Chapter 18: Afterwards: Get together in Rock Ferry, Wirral,
England 301

Appendix 303

Index 309

Chapter One

Simon and Penny in Belgium

Simon is my son and Penny his wife of 20 years. They have always been very supportive of me and all of my mad schemes. Both of them are very good company, together and separately. As well as my motherly love for them, I also like them both very much. I'm glad that they wanted to come and share in this adventure.

Day 1: April 21st 2014

"We would like to join you on the first leg of your trip if that is okay with you" said my son Simon. They wanted to come and see me off on my travels from home, and spend a few days with me in Antwerp. I was delighted.

"Don't worry about the taxi to the station, I'll see to that" I said. I wanted to start off in style, so I secretly hired an executive car.

Well, this was it. I gave my Cairo a cuddle, said goodbye to Paula, gathered my luggage and got into the car. The driver and his wife had both bought into my dream. So off we went, to pick up Si and Penny. Their road was quite narrow so the car had to turn around while I knocked on their door.

Si came out. "Where's the taxi, Ma?"

As it arrived I said, "Well actually this is it". The look on his face was priceless. Well, we had to at least start in style. Penny was similarly amazed. We arrived at Lime Street station relaxed and more than a little excited.

Our first train journey was to London Euston, then on to St. Pancras for the Eurostar to the Continent. I felt like I was a traveller embarking on 'The Grand Tour', in the 1900s. I was already beginning to worry about the luggage on the walk between stations. We had coffee, well, tea in my case, and sat and stared at St. Pancras and its beautiful glass roof. The station was very busy with myriads of people on the move, never still for a moment. We were also serenaded by various people playing the piano, installed in the main hall for just such a purpose. We booked in for the train and went to the Departure Lounge, a flight experience without the flight.

The Eurostar was very impressive and comfortable and once we got going, very fast. We arrived in France within an hour, then on to our destination of Brussels. The last leg of the journey was a local train up to Antwerp where we arrived early evening. Not bad for just one day's travel.

A little background:

'Antwerp is a port city on the River Scheldt in the Flanders region of Belgium. A region forever associated with the battlefields of WW1. The

old town is the location of the Grote Markt, displaying many examples of Flemish architecture. It is thought that the name comes from 'an't werf' (on the wharf), but there is also another line of thought that it is 'aan't warp' (at the warp, man-made hill or river deposit)'.

There is of course, a folklore reason for the name. There is a legend about a Giant named Antigoon who lived near the river exacting tolls from all boatmen who passed. Those who did not pay had one of their hands severed and thrown into the river.

'The Town was thought to have been settled from the 4th century. Antwerp's golden age was likened to the "Age of exploration" and during the 16th century the town, now a city, grew to be the second largest European city north of the Alps. The 80 years war broke out in 1568 leading to the sacking of the city by the Spanish. The city then changed hands various times, to the Dutch, to Napoleon, the Germans in WWII and finally became Belgium.'

Antwerp station was a stunningly beautiful marble building, and when we came outside we immediately fell in love with the city. It had a vibrancy about it, similar to that of Barcelona or Venice. We stood outside the station for quite some time just to look and take it all in. Even in that small area there were lots of historical buildings, the entrance to the Zoo, a pop-up restaurant, people on bicycles and a hubbub of voices. Wonderful.

Now to find where we are staying. The owner of the B&B was Rob, originally from Holland but settled many years in Antwerp. A small but perfectly formed guest house with just two bedrooms and a sitting and dining area. After registering and being greeted with a drink, we went for a walk through the city in search of the recommended restaurant. A little story in regard to the restaurant: White Asparagus is a delicacy of the area, but Simon, not being a lover of vegetables, decided to go with the only thing he recognised on the menu, steak. Unfortunately when it came, it was raw, hadn't noticed the tartare bit, but being so hungry, ate it anyway.

After the good food, full and tired, we went back to our 'home' for a good sleep. We unpacked just what was necessary, then headed to bed ready for sightseeing the next morning. After all, this was still Day 1, a tantalising hint of the adventures to come.

Day 2

An excellent breakfast greeted us when we awoke, followed by a leisurely getting ready for our sightseeing day.

We went to the old town section to the Cathedral square. What a view; the Cathedral stood proud over the square, so imposing with its very tall spire. Then having done all the normal touristy things outside of it – you know – a photograph here, a photograph there, a photograph against the church backdrop: "Are you sure I am in shot?" "Not too close". "Get my best side" etc, etc, we finally went inside.

Hanging from all corners were paintings by Paul Rubens depicting the life of Christ from the Nativity, through the teaching and healing times to the crucifixion. What a treat. We spent quite some time in there, standing in awe of what we were seeing.

Back outside, we again took in the view of the square and its many old guild houses each with a golden roof adornment. We decided that it was time for a drink so went to a bar called Den Engel and sat outside and surveyed the ever-changing human scenery. Simon with his blond - beer that is, Penny with her wine and for me, a cup of tea. We sat watching the flow of people across the square, some perhaps on business errands, some tourists like us, some just passing the time of day. Amazing how quickly an hour goes by.

Back to Antigoon, the not so friendly giant, who terrorised the town. Legend has it that some Roman soldiers caught him and he was killed by a young hero named Silvius Brabo who cut off the giant's hand and threw it into the river. There are monuments to this in various locations; his hand lay in the main shopping street. There was also a large fountain in the shape of the giant with water spurting out of the stump:

and a statue of the giant and the soldiers at Steen Castle. I took more photographs, of course.

From the castle, which is now just a replica, we walked along the promenade to the dock area, to the MAS building. This was now a museum which had a 10th storey observation platform with views across the whole city. The areas surrounding the elevators had art work and video installations, interesting and some more than a little bizarre. From the top we saw a crane in the dock and on closer inspection saw that it was a barge with a bar on it. Guess where we went next; it was thirsty work all that sightseeing.

So there we were, on the deck of an old barge, housing a full sized crane, floating in the Napoleon Dock, complete with chickens, lots of plants and of course, the bar. Quite surreal. As if that wasn't enough, a mobile bar (one of those bicycle things propelled by leg power), pulled up. The lads in the party jumped off, peed over the dock wall and pedalled off again, singing loudly. We laughed; that certainly was not a sight you saw every day.

More sightseeing; on to the Town Hall, a most beautiful building.

Europe does have the most spectacular Government buildings, usually with an equally beautiful fountain to complete the scene. It's funny; you always think that you have so much time to do everything then suddenly the day is over. So now to eat; we were recommended to go to the Boura restaurant, a good choice, very good meal, no mistakes this time, then a slow walk home. There was just time for a round of drinks in the lounge area and then to bed.

Day 3

This was ' moving on day', the first of many for me. A good breakfast was enjoyed by all, then we got ready, packed and made sure that we had collected all of our belongings. We wandered slowly through the city, looking particularly at the district we had been staying in. It was one of the ethnic areas with large numbers of people of African descent, and this was reflected in the local shops, particularly the hairdressers advertising their services, hair styles and so on. I found it really interesting.

We got the local train to Brussels, wishing Antwerp a silent but very fond farewell. Si, Penny and I would be going our separate ways, they to continue their holiday with friends in Kent and me, well I went to Germany, to Cologne, a new country, new city, and a new part of the adventure.

The train journey was good and I spent my time talking to a 6'7" hunk of a man who kindly helped me with my luggage. He was good company and we each talked about our plans for the future. Time flew past. Crossed the border into Germany.

I arrived at the station and the first view on stepping outside was the magnificent Cathedral. Breathtaking.

Some information for you.

'Cologne is a 2000 year old city spanning both sides of the River Rhine, in the Federal State of North-Rhine Westphalia. It is the 4th largest city in Germany, founded around 38BC, and was originally the capital of the Roman Province of the Interior. It was one of the most important trade routes between East and West Europe, and a leading member of the Hanseatic League.

Following heavy bombing during WWII restoration of the city was begun in 1947. This included the rebuilding of many of the Romanesque churches and other landmarks. Reconstruction continued up until the 1990s, and included a new flood control system. The city is characterised by some famous monumental buildings such as the city gates, medieval houses, various bridges, churches and the Cathedral. In more recent times, new museums and high-rise structures have been added, and as with other modern cities, it has grown exponentially.'

But first things first, taxi to the hotel I had chosen, which was in the Altstadt, the old town area, on the river's edge. A nice place with an attached outdoor restaurant. And the river, well it was the mystical Rhine. I remembered stories from my childhood about the Rhine, the Lorelei rock and the mermaids – not that Cologne was anywhere near there, but the association was enough to conjure up the magic of the river.

I checked in, rested in my room for a while, then went for some food. Duly fed and watered I went for a stroll around the old town area. There were lots of pavement cafes, very lively place teaming with people. I walked over to the Cathedral again, which was closer than I had realised and took photographs of the outside. Regardless of the time of day, the area was always full of people milling about, some like me photographing everything in sight, and being entertained by the various street acts that are there in abundance.

Night was slowly falling, so it was back to the hotel.

I snuggled into my bed and watched a little TV. I can understand some German, well, a little. And so to sleep.

Day 4

Another 'moving on day', although the train was an overnight sleeper and not due until 10 p.m. I decided to fill every minute of my day. I started off with a good breakfast - I can't do anything until I have eaten. So, what to do? A mini-cruise down (or is it up) the Rhine was a must and as the terminal was right opposite the hotel, so a cruise it was. I sat out on the top deck and surveyed the scene. I have always loved rivers, the sights, the sounds, smells and feel very at home near them, especially as the River Mersey was on my doorstep in Rock Ferry and was part of my upbringing. The scenery was very varied, one bank filled with greenery, the other with buildings old and new.

In the distance I could see a cable car system which crossed the river. *That looks interesting* I thought. *Wonder where that goes from?*. A word of caution here, it was just that sort of thinking that saw me up a mountain in Nepal, and on the end of a sled with five Huskies in the Arctic Circle.

Well, it was actually from the Zoo which was quite a long way from where I was, and I didn't know how to get there.

On returning to dry land, I decided to go back and photograph the interior of the Cathedral. It was still only lunch time, would you believe, so now what to do. I wandered about, then saw a little tourist-type train, you know, the ones that look like large sized children's toys. Guess where it went to, oh joy, the Zoo. So off I went, great idea but with one little snag, it bounced and clattered the whole way. I had to check that my teeth and bones were still with me when we arrived, but, you know, it was fun.

I found the terminal for the cable car and queued to await my turn. Apparently this was the only one that not only crossed a river, but a motorway as well.

I didn't get off at the other side due to time constraints, but I really enjoyed the trip. My faithful camera ever at the ready. I went back to the hotel, had a meal, sat and watched the world go by, then ordered a taxi to go to the station.

Here, however, was the beginning of things going awry. The station was quite near to the hotel, but up a number of steps and as previously stated I had a lot of luggage and so needed help. The driver arrived, did not help, and when I told him where I was going, he was really annoyed.

"The station over there?"

"Yes" I said.

"I have waited nearly an hour in the queue for a job, and now it's over there".

"Sorry, but my luggage is very heavy". At this point I felt sorry for him, but then, in a very mocking voice he mimicked me. I was appalled; I have never experienced such rudeness anywhere I have travelled, long or short taxi journey. There goes his tip. I was very surprised, as he was from a background that was reputed to revere their elders, which I was by several decades. Sadly this was to be the first of many appalling taxi driver encounters, although thankfully not on every occasion.

I arrived at the station platform in good time and settled to wait for the overnight sleeper train to Copenhagen. I started talking to an English guy on his way to a birthday party celebration in Denmark. Ten minutes before the train was due to arrive, an announcement was made, that neither of us could understand. A young Thai lady appeared and told us she had found a station worker who had said that due to flooding on the line, our train was being diverted to Dortmund. Such a scrabble with all of the luggage over to another platform where station staff sorted tickets and so on for us to go to Dortmund.

Arrived there about midnight. Ah well, these things happen, and happen they did because every time we thought the train was coming, it turned out to be another delay. The train finally arrived at 03.30. *At last*, I thought, *I should be able to get into my bunk and sleep the rest of the way.* But no, we had to change at Hamburg, two hours away so no real sleep.

Arrived at Hamburg, five hours behind schedule to wait for the next Copenhagen train. I met up again with the young lady and we travelled the rest of the way together. We did not see our other companion, but we hoped he got to his party on time.

Day 5

We travelled through German rural areas and up to the German/Danish border. Once through, saw we were surrounded by water, mmm, interesting, now what. Ahead of us was a docked boat, and to my amazement, three coaches of the train were taken on board for the 40 minute crossing.

We had to go up on deck, but it was a good opportunity to get some food. The whole thing was bizarre. *Now*, I thought, *that's a first*.

Let me tell you about my firsts. Some 20 years ago I suffered from depression and one of my self-help remedies was to take pleasure in things that I realised I was experiencing for the first time, big or small, important or frivolous did not matter; it was just the fact of it being a first. I have done it ever since. It's a great feeling to know that there are still so many things to discover year on year.

Anyway, back to the boat. After feeding our faces, it was time to feed our minds and enjoy the beautiful scenery. Photographic opportunities galore. Then it was time to get back on to the train ready to disembark, and continue the rail journey to Copenhagen.

Chapter 2

Gill in Scandinavia

I have known Gill since the 1990s, first as a work colleague and later as a good friend. We have shared in a number of travels, Spain and Sweden amongst others, and we are also quite adept in 'putting the world, according to us, to rights'. We have always enjoyed a good long chat.

Day 5

Arrived finally at Copenhagen station, not as frazzled as I had expected to be, excitement being a wonderful thing to keep you awake. I was meeting Gill at the airport hotel, so a taxi was my first priority; well actually the 'Ladies' came first, as always. Cannot let a toilet go by; never know when its use will become necessary. All of a certain age will know this. A nice taxi driver took me out to the hotel. I always ask for a card if the driver has treated me well, so that I can use them again during my stay. Arrived at the room and Gill was already there. Big hugs all around, and a cup of tea.

A little story: I played this scenario out when meeting up with each of my friends. After the hellos, I would point to a small piece of luggage and say, very seriously "before we go anywhere, I need to instruct you in the use of this, my first-aid box". Well, what amazing friends I have, with no hesitation, it was a case of okay, let's see how everything works. It wasn't any such thing. Lucky for me, they all understood my off-beat sense of humour. However, I did notice that in many of the major train stations there were very comprehensive first-aid areas. Very comforting to know for anyone with any medical problems.

After a short rest, we unpacked just what was needed, then went back into Copenhagen centre. The Metro station was just around the corner, and as you can imagine the trains were frequent, very clean and fast. We walked first to the harbour.

What a feast for the eyes, ears and nose, in fact all of the senses. We loved the vibrancy of everything, the colours, the reflections, the street bands and of course, the food.

We had Smorresbrod for our evening meal, really enormous open sandwiches on a platter, made from several varieties of meats and fish. We then wandered around for a few hours then back to the hotel. I had a relaxing bath, then bed. It was good not to worry about having to change trains in the middle of the night, so I slept soundly.

Day 6

We had a healthy breakfast; what else would you expect in Denmark? We then went back to the centre, our enthusiasm for the harbour area undiminished. More wandering, and yes, I did take lots of photographs. We watched a young man making waffles of which we had to partake; they were delicious. After a while we went on the Hop-on-Hop-off (from here onwards forever christened 'HoHo' buses; well, we had a laugh on them).

We saw on the way, a Guards Company out exercising their horses. The route took us out to the area where the statue of 'The Little Mermaid' sat, as immortalised by H.C. Anderson.

The statue was so small and her wistful glance to the land, almost heartbreaking. I felt happy and sad at the same time; it was so beautifully done.

There was a lovely park area there, and as expected many tourists milling about, chattering loudly like flocks of birds. Once back at the start of the route, we went on a boat trip around the harbour.

We laughed about our funny incident, which happened on the Metro on our way into the centre. When the train stopped I got off but Gill was delayed by other passengers and the doors started to close. In something reminiscent of Wonder Woman, she put her hands in the gap and opened the doors just wide enough to jump off. The train was some minutes before it moved off again. We found out later that the whole circuit was driverless and so we probably held up the entire system. Oops.

We went to a decidedly dodgy looking cafe where wafts of the various smells were not all of food, but an experience nonetheless. After our meal we went back to the main station to get the Metro back to the hotel. In a square nearby was a wall with black flaps which, when lifted up, revealed various colours. The idea being that passers-by could lift up what they chose, thus making a pattern. It was called 'The Happy Wall', so we, along with others, made our patterns too.

Back in our room it was time to pack for the next phase. We were moving on to Sweden. A bit of a performance, because this section involved two flights and I had far too much luggage, so we had to share everything between us to make its weight acceptable. I have to say, Gill was a superb packer.

Day 7

We had already decided that we wanted to cross over the Oresund Bridge, which had come to our attention in the TV thriller 'The Bridge', which we both loved. In fact we were both big fans of the Scandinavian noir type thrillers.

'The Oresund Bridge is a cable style bridge plus tunnel. It is a combined road and rail structure linking Denmark and Sweden. At nearly 12 km overall, part of the complex is underground, surfacing at an artificial

island, to avoid interfering with the air traffic from Copenhagen airport. Construction started in 1995 and it opened to traffic in 2000.'

We hired our taxi, and the driver was so helpful and spoke English, as did everyone we met. He took us to a vantage point for an excellent view of the sound and the bridge. We took many photos, then continued the trip. The first section, as stated, was underground, the approach being like that of the Mersey Tunnel connecting Birkenhead to Liverpool, and when you came to the surface you were already on the bridge. The taxi slowed so that we could take more photos. It was a real thrill which we both enjoyed. The bridge was the connecting arm between Copenhagen and Malmo. We duly arrived at Malmo rail station. We were now in Sweden.

Our plan was to travel first by rail to Gothenburg and then on to two connecting flights up to Kiruna in the far north of Sweden. But back to Malmo. We didn't have much time before the train so were only able to see the immediate area around the station, and a small town square.

However we did revisit Malmo on the way back to Denmark, so more details later.

We returned to the station to reserve our seats on the train, very important to do, in all of Europe, and Asia, wherever possible. We had a good trip up to Gothenburg, chatting and looking out at the rolling countryside as we passed by. Everything was so clean, even the fields. We had four hours to spare on arrival so decided to go and see the 22ft. tall Poseidon statue, which had been made to celebrate the city's 300 year anniversary. I had seen this once before, in 1989, when I was searching for my Swedish relatives, and had travelled with my friend David L. Funny how things are; I had remembered it as being much larger then, but even so, it was still very imposing. It has a commanding position, in Goteplatsen square, at the top of the main boulevard, looking down over the city.

The Avenyen was very busy, with lots of people, again a mix of locals and tourists, with the noise and general hubbub that you would expect from a city, especially one as nice as this one. There, by a small park, was a South American Pipe Band, which I am sure I had last seen playing in Chester; I recognised the main player. We stopped at an outdoor cafe for a drink and cake, then went off to find the bus for the airport.

A slight hitch occurred here: I had inadvertently packed my toiletries into my hand luggage; as I had said, reducing the amount of said luggage was a nightmare, so consequently I had it all confiscated. Purely my fault, so take heed all ye fellow travellers. Firstly the flight was up to Stockholm, with a 40 minute layover, then on to Kiruna. We arrived late at night and saw the lights of the town reflecting in the snow as we came in to land.

The town was in the far north of the Swedish Lapland and known for the huge iron ore mine and underground visitor centre. Known to everyone it seemed, but us. We thought we were going to an isolated village with the Sami people, reindeer and huskies, but still it did not disappoint. The city shared a long history with the indigenous Sami peoples, with over 6000 years of settlement. The area became a city in 1900, and very quickly became a major mining area.

Due to its position north of the Arctic Circle, the city was known to have a harsh climate, thus the reason for all the cold weather gear we took with us, and also experienced both the midnight sun and the polar night. The mine was established in 1890, and the Narvik railway was built in 1898. During the first decades of the city's existence no roads connected it to the outside world. The only connection was the railway, and in the summer, by boat along the river to Jukkasjarvi, later made famous by the building of the Ice Hotel in 1990, and every year since, and from there by foot. In 2007 the town centre had to be moved due to ground deformations caused by the mining, then again in 2014. Tourism had become an important source of income in both summer and winter.

But back to the airport. There was a minibus to meet us and the other passengers, mostly mine workers, and we were given a tour of the town as we were the last to be dropped off. It was all coldness and silence, the town that was, not the people. We booked into our hotel and ate the lovely supper that had been left for us. Such a nice welcome. And so it was to bed after a very full day of travelling. There were to be many of those on the rest of the trip.

Day 8

We woke to a good breakfast, put our cold weather gear on and went for a wander around the town area. Unfortunately we were between seasons so many things were closed, or only open on certain days which sadly were not the days we were there, such as the trip into the mine. A shame, we would have liked that. On our way to the Tourist Information office, Gill casually but insistently mentioned that she would have liked more snow;

must say there was enough for me, but we were talking here about an intrepid traveller around Iceland, so I could see what she meant.

We managed to book for a husky sled ride. The owner picked us up at our hotel and took us out to the centre. Our guide was to be Jan, originally from Slovakia. Great bloke, we really liked him. Changed into our wet weather clothes and were allotted wellington type boots. Tres chic. Jan got the dogs ready and harnessed up to the sled, a wooden frame with a reindeer fur thrown over it. Reindeer were used for many purposes especially by the Sami peoples, for transport, food and clothing.

Back to the sled. Gill got on first, then me and then we were off. The speed of travel was quite surprising so we really had to hold on, a little difficult when photograph taking was the priority. As it was so late into the season the snow and ice had begun to melt, not a problem in the forest areas, but the lake was a different matter, just a bit hairy. I asked when the season ended, and was told airily, "two weeks ago". Oh. However, we were perfectly safe and felt reassured with Jan and his expert handling of the dogs.

We stopped at a hut and were treated to a hot drink and muffins. Turns out that Jan had spent some time at the Villmarkssenter Centre in Tromso, Norway in 2010, where I had done the Husky Challenge Charity Run in 2008, (but that's another story). I mentioned the names of my dog team, two of whom he had worked with, and he told me that one of my lead dogs, Yentna, had had some puppies. Such a nice guy, we had a really good chat about living so far north into the Arctic Circle amongst other topics.

Then it was time to track back through the forest to the Sledding centre. Once changed we were given a hot drink and another amazing treat. We were taken to see some puppies, beautiful little blue-eyed cuties.

A very good day. Back at the hotel, we looked look through our photos, had some chit-chat then went for a Jacuzzi in the attic of the building. Food then sleep.

Day 9

We woke to a great volume of noise. "I don't believe this. All the surrounding houses must have put their bins outside our hotel" said Gill.

The noise got steadily louder so in the end she got up and looked out of the window,, Well, her bed was the nearest. Her smile lit up the room. "It's a snow plough, and better yet, it is still snowing".

Oh great I thought from under the covers.

"How GREAT" she said.

Can you believe that 30cms of snow had fallen over night, the most in one night since the 1970s. I blame Gill for it; she wished it on us and Kiruna. Ah well, breakfast then snowballs at 20 paces, and on to our goal for that day, to visit the Sami museum and the local Kyrka (church).

'Sami people are nomadic indigenous tribes of the north and live across Lapland (or Sapmi) which covers part of four countries, Norway, Sweden, Finland and Russia. They speak a number of languages, including that of the Uralic linguistic group. Traditionally they made their living from herding reindeer, and supported themselves through fishing, livestock farming and hunting, but in more recent times in public sector jobs, travel and tourist areas. Land rights battles had been on-going in many of the countries, but seemed at last to be coming down in favour of the Sami people.'

We enjoyed our visit to the museum. The displays showed many different aspects of Sami life, old photographs and actual items used in their once nomadic life. Some people have now settled in housing areas.

We went back to our hotel, and later decided to go out to Jukkisjarvi on the local bus. We had to wait 30 minutes at the bus stop, so we decided to play I-spy, much to the amusement of a local lady. Well it made the time go quicker, and made us forget the waiting and the cold. It reminded me of family holidays and long journeys in the car, interminably long when you are 12. The bus came, with a very helpful female driver who told us about the timetables and what to see.

As our time was limited we decided to get off at the location of the world famous Ice Hotel, newly built each year.

Unfortunately, as it was at the end of the season, the structure was abandoned and melting. It looked so sad. When I did the Husky Challenge, the visit to the Ice Hotel was the part that I missed out on, so it was good to be able to go, albeit six years later. Back on the bus to Kiruna and then a walk back to our hotel. Oh, did I mention, it was my Birthday this day? So a happy face all day long. It was time to pack again, a very early flight awaiting us.

Day 10

We got up at 4 a.m. for the pick up to the airport. So cold. No problems this time at the check in, and we had a good flight down to Stockholm. We left our luggage at the train station as it was much too early to book into the hotel. Some sustenance, then as the city woke up we went to find the HoHo bus. What a treat; no, I don't just mean the trip, but the driver. What a gorgeous guy, with an amazing smile and the longest eyelashes I had ever seen.

'Stockholm is the capital of Sweden, surrounded by 14 islands and more than 50 bridges. It is on the Baltic Sea Archipelago at the mouth of Lake Malaren. A settlement since the Stone Age, and had been recognised as a city since 1252. The old town area was built from the 13th century onwards and was linked to the Hanseatic League. Daylight hours in the winter are short, the city being located near the 60th latitude. There is little heavy industry, 85% of jobs being in the service industry. The city has many museums, such as the Vasa maritime museum, Skansen, and the Nobel museum dedicated to Alfred Noble (Nobel Prize), amongst many others. There are also many art galleries, theatres and top ranking universities such as the Karolinska Institute, and of course, the Abba Museum.'

We enjoyed our trip around the city, took lots of photographs, then later went on a boat cruise around the harbour and to some of the islands.

There are many small islands that make up Stockholm, many of which are inhabited by one or two families. What beautiful vistas they have to wake up to each day. Later we walked back to the station, picked up our luggage and got another HoHo bus to our hotel, well hostel actually.

This was a boat in the harbour, in which we had a cabin as our room. Interesting experience, especially the half bath, half shower. After a wander around our 'ship', we went on a small ferry over to Skansen for Walpurgis Night, known as 'Mischief Night'. We ate in a good restaurant, then went into the theme park. Skansen is a large open air museum showing Swedish life through the centuries, with houses recreated from various times and areas, handicrafts and people in costume who wandered about, ready to answer any questions.

However, this was night time and none of the exhibits were open, so our more comprehensive sightseeing had to be reserved for a day time visit. We made a mistake in our wardrobe choice and did not wear our fleeces under our jackets, so consequently nearly froze to death. Well, slight exaggeration, but it was very cold. No snow there but cold air travels down from the north, so we should have known better. Just managed to brave the temperature long enough to take a photograph overlooking the city.

We got the ferry back to the harbour and our hostel, and the warmth. We were very tired after a long but full day. Fell gratefully into our bunks.

Day 11 May 1st

A leisurely morning after a good sleep. We spent some time planning the next part of our Scandinavian adventure, a train trip to Karlstad. I always thought that my family were originally from there, but later found out it was near Karlshamn, a place called Hallaryd. We walked to the station to get our tickets ready for the next day. Next, it was back to the HoHos; this time we got a very flamboyant driver with a great sense of humour. Not too many people on the bus, so we had a laugh with him. Also had a laugh trying to take selfies, in the form of reflections in various windows, with some strange distorted results. More sightseeing; we were impressed with the Royal Palace complex and the immaculately turned out guardsmen, and then it was time to eat.

As this was May 1st, there were many May Day demonstrations, flag flying, fists punching the air, whole families airing their views. All very orderly and well-behaved, but also enthusiastic with bands and singing.

We found a restaurant, then it was back for an early night, but not before our own discussions and putting the world to rights. Another early start was required, but thankfully not a 4 a.m. touch.

Day 12

An early train, not too busy, and much easier because we had booked seats. Once our luggage was stowed, we sat back for a restful journey. A young couple got on and sat opposite us. The young man had the sort of face you normally only see in Pre-Raphaelite paintings, we were fascinated. I tried to take a sneaky photograph, but it didn't really work; served me right.

Fortunately the new hotel was opposite the station, so we didn't have to move the luggage very far, which had already become the bane of my life. We had a walk around, once registered, then we caught a local bus out to an outdoor museum called Marienborg Skogan, a sort of mini Skansen. There was one of those small trains that trundle around the area, so we went on a very bumpy ride through the trees - here go the teeth again. It was a small, but nice enough place. The return bus took us through a number of housing estates and shopping areas. I really liked using the local transport as it gave me a much stronger connection with the Country.

Later we had a meal at the hotel, then went out for an evening stroll. Funny place, Karlstad; there didn't seem to be a lot going on, but of course it could have been happening elsewhere and we didn't know it, being strangers and all. One thing we did find was the Peace Monument in the middle of the main square, erected in memory of the peaceful dissolution of the union between Sweden and Norway in 1905. Unveiled in 1955, it showed a woman with a broken sword, and at its foundation, the following words 'Feud breeds hatred between people, peace promotes public understanding'.

Day 13

We took a taxi out to Lake Vannen.

'The largest lake in Sweden, located in the provinces of Vastergotland, Dalsland and Varmland in the south-west of Sweden. It was formed after the last ice age, and was mentioned in the Old English epic story Beowulf. It covers 5,655 Km, is 89 km deep, and has many different fish species, important for industry around the Lake.'

It was about seven km out from the town. We were there quite some time taking photos of the beautiful views. Later the driver took us to some old buildings that had survived the 1865 fire.

As this was a moving on day, we went back to the hotel for our luggage, ready for our train journey back to Malmo, with just one change at Gothenburg. We arrived early evening, hungry, so went for the fast food option. We were both tired, checked into our hotel, straight to our room, read for a while and then bed. Oh, did I mention, also washed our 'smalls', a chore to be repeated in each country. Well, I wasn't able to take an endless supply, and going 'commando' wasn't always an option.

Day 14 May 4th

We planned our day over breakfast. As we were both fans of the various TV Scandinavian Thrillers that had been aired over the past years, we decided to go on a 'fan' trail. Firstly we went to Lund.

Lund is a typical little Swedish town, but with an amazing Cathedral housing an old Astronomical Clock. Twice in the day, at 12 noon and 3 p.m. the pipers sounded and three Wise Men rotated around the face to pay homage to the Mary and Child statue.

We spent quite some time in the church, there was a lot to see besides the clock. The vicar had a look of Jesus, as depicted in many paintings, and a red-cloaked choir sang in the background. An interesting and enjoyable experience. Lund itself was very quiet, but had some interesting buildings.

From there, back on the train to Ystad. We went to the old town and followed in the footsteps of the character, Kurt Wallender; we had a drink in the cafe depicted in the programme, proper tourists, and went to see some of the other buildings shown in the programme, such as the police station and the area supposedly outside of his house. We even saw a train named after him. I love it when fiction meets fact. We walked along by the harbour area, and back to our train. We really liked Ystad. We had our evening meal back in Malmo at the Mello Yellow cafe on the town square.

Day 15

We travelled out to the vantage point, on the Swedish side, to see the Oresund Bridge. It was very impressive from whichever side you viewed it, truly magnificent. It was a beautiful, warm day and sun glinted off the moving water making golden patterns. We just sat, relaxed and enjoyed the scene.

From there it was back to Copenhagen, this time by train. The train travelled underneath the road section of the bridge. We booked into our hotel, then went off to continue our 'fan' trail, this time in Denmark. Firstly we went to the Danish Parliament building, as seen in the drama 'Borgan'. We were actually able to walk through a tunnel from the back to the front of the building; can you imagine doing that at Downing Street?

We decided to visit the Tivoli Gardens again.

We watched a mime show at the Peacock Theatre and then just soaked up the atmosphere. The evening was spent packing ready for moving on the next day.

Day 16

Off to the station for a parting of the ways, Gill to the airport and me firstly to Hamburg and then via Cologne to connect with the overnight train to Warsaw. The train was called the Jan Kipura; don't these trains have wonderful names? Fortunately this train arrived on time and I was shown to my single berth without incident. It was a good journey and I slept well.

Chapter 3

Sandra and Helen in Warsaw, Poland

I have known Sandra, and through her, Helen, for over 20 years. Sandra and I used to meet at the bus stop on the way to work for months before we realised not only did we live in the same road, but four doors from each other. Friends from then on, who shared not only a love of travelling, but also of having a good laugh on the top deck of the bus, much to the annoyance of the early morning stiff, formal sleepy heads.

Day 17

The Polish countryside was quite a contrast to what I had seen in Sweden and Denmark, and Germany come to that; much more rural. I got a taxi from the station, out to the old town area. As the driver was getting my luggage from the boot, another taxi pulled up behind and out stepped Sandra and Helen. So you can imagine the noise, whoops of delight and kisses and hugs all around. How's that for timing. The two taxi drivers were bemused.

'Warsaw is Poland's capital, standing on the River Fistula and roughly midway between the Baltic and the Carpathian mountains. The first historical references date back to 1313. It became known as Phoenix City because of its survival through many conflicts and invasions. In 1939, invasion of Poland by Nazi Germany saw the beginning of WWII as other western nations had pacts to defend Poland. The city was 85% destroyed, including the historic castle and old town area. After the war, whilst under communist rule much of the city was rebuilt, just as it had been pre-war. Pope John Paul 11 was an inhabitant of Warsaw, as were Chopin and Marie Curie. The city boasts many fine university faculties, theatres and museums.'

We caught our first glimpse of the old town; we liked it already.

We found the doorway to the building where our flat was to be. Unfortunately I had arrived later than expected, so had missed the owner Taduez. He fortunately had made a further arrangement with his father-in-law to bring us the key when we got there. Aren't mobile phones wonderful, so easy to sort things out. Father-in-law duly arrived, a really nice guy called Nicholas. He spoke English and was really helpful with all of our questions. Apart from please, thank you and of course hello, we only knew our own language; we felt very inadequate.

This was to be the first flat of the trip, and we were very impressed. One tiny problem was that the flat was on the third floor, up nine sets of stairs.

The first time up I couldn't speak on reaching our door, but after a couple of days it was like having the best ever gym workout. This was a taste of what was to come, stairs everywhere. But, the view was amazing.

The flat overlooked the old town square, complete with outdoor cafes, and a mermaid statue. It made every single stair worth the trip.

Once we had unpacked and had a bit of a rest, it was time to go out exploring. We went for a walk around the square and found ice creams in every variety you could imagine, so of course we had to try them out. The girls wandered off whilst I stopped to photograph a church door on the Jesuit church of the Gracious Mother of God.

I stood on the steps to line up the shot, when from behind me an Italian couple went up, opened the door, went in and left the door open. Hmm. I went up, shut the door and realigned my shot. Unbeknownst to me, a Japanese tourist had joined me on the steps, camera in hand. Before either of us could press the shutter button, the door opened and the same couple came out again, and guess what, left the door open and walked off.

I couldn't help myself, I said loudly "shut the b****y door".

There was a very slight pause, then a voice beside me said "no worries, I'll shut the b****y door". We both laughed, took our photographs and went our separate ways. International incident averted.

I caught up with the girls, still laughing.

We spent some happy hours wandering around the old town streets. We just loved the style of the old buildings, the noise, the people going about their business, whether it be for work or pleasure, and the babble of the many different accents. Later we went for a meal in a nice little place just off the square. We walked slowly back towards the flat. Suddenly from around a corner, came a rather large Panda, on roller skates, carrying a shopping bag and skating at full tilt on the very wet pavement that the weather had just provided. We stared from beneath our umbrellas.

We looked at each other to ascertain that we had just seen what we thought we had seen, and that it was not down to the wine imbibed at the restaurant. We had a good chat, relived the day's events, then bed.

Day 18

Time to hit the HoHos; no self-respecting city is without one. We went around the various sights of the city, took in some of the newer parts, including a large war memorial dedicated to the freedom fighters of WWll, taking photographs all the way. We decided later we would go out to a Jewish Cemetery. We had quite a wait for the bus, so guess what we played? Of course, I-Spy. It made the girls laugh as was the case with Gill in Sweden. They had not played it for years, reminded us all of our childhoods. Amazing what can amuse when you have time to 'sit and stare'.

We went on to the Rising Museum, a commemoration of the 1944 uprising against Nazi occupation. There were many artefacts, video enactments and lots of in-depth information. Back on another bus, we travelled through the leafy Foreign Embassy areas, the modern business areas and the upmarket housing areas. We also went through some of the less salubrious areas, the grey blocks of workers flats, throwbacks from the Soviet era.

Still, it all added to the unique feeling of the city, each area was worthy of our interest. We had to walk back from the new town area, as we were informed we were at the end terminus for the bus. Oh dear, lost.

Fortunately the driver set us on the right road, but it was a long walk. A little compensation though; we found another ice cream shop near the old town square. So there we sat, cornets in hand, watching the world go by, and steeling ourselves to climb Everest, well the nine flights of stairs, for a freshen up before our evening meal. We found a good Indian restaurant to partake of our meal. Mine was very hot -oops, I really should have learnt the various terminologies for what was hot, and what was not. We had a relaxed evening, lots of talking, sharing of photo images, and later watched people come and go from our window overlooking the square, and finally to bed.

Day 19

We visited the Royal Palace Museum, beautifully restored with much to see inside, and also the surrounding square with the usual mix of buskers, street artists, tourists, local people and us. We went into St John's Church.

    We later sat outside and ate our sandwiches and just happened to see a giant Panda sitting on a wall. Oh joy, now we knew we had not been hallucinating. It wasn't the Panda, but the roller skates that convinced us. I saw all manner of animals and historical figures, often painted silver, in the cities, who became animated, and very happy, when you gave them your bronze, silver or gold.

The day went by very quickly and before we knew it, we were back in a small Italian restaurant eating again. Our experience of Polish food was to take place later in the afternoon. We found a very rustic cafe and enjoyed polish pancakes, and talked to the owners about their lives and Poland. As with all things, the time went far too quickly, so, it was back for a stroll around the square, and bed.

Day 20

We packed ready for a half-move. What's that, do I hear you asking? Well, we had to move out of the flat, but because my plans had changed, I was still going to be in Poland an extra day. So it was off to the airport hotel, to await flights for Sandra and Helen back to England, and for me, to Russia. The original idea was to go to Moscow, via Belarus, but due to maintenance works on the line, I couldn't get a ticket. Well, that was the official line anyway. Still, more time for sightseeing.

We thanked Tadeuz, who kindly let us leave our luggage at the flat before we went on to the airport, and also for the use of the place. We said we were sorry that we hadn't met him, but that we had enjoyed meeting his father-in-law. So, to our last sights of Warsaw. We went on a small road train around the city. As with the one in Cologne this was also a bit of a bone shaker. This was to be the 'train' journey shared by me, Sandra and Helen.

There were lots of marches going on, again peacefully, the changing of the guards at the castle, more street artists and the general clamour of people. Our goal for the day was to visit the Marie Curie museum.

'Marie Sklodowska Curie was a Polish and naturalised French Physicist and Chemist, and pioneer researcher in radioactivity. Discovered Radium and Polonium. She was the first woman to win a Nobel Prize and the only woman to win twice, (1903 Physics prize with husband Pierre and Henri Becquerel, and in 1911 for Chemistry). She began her scientific training in 1891 aged 24. During WW1 established the first mobile military radiological units. She died aged 66 years.'

The museum was very interesting with a mocked up laboratory, equipment and fragments of her family life, including many photographs. I first heard of her whilst at school, so there was much excitement as an historical figure suddenly became flesh and blood and a real person emerged. I have found this to be true in other situations, such as having seen first-hand, the sap running from a rubber tree in the jungles of Brunei, originally having seen pictures in a school geography book. When things that you never think you will see for real unfold before your eyes, the effect is magical. More food, more ice cream, then back for our luggage, and on to the airport.

Had a nice meal with the girls, then back to the room to make sure all my packing was in order for the flight the next day. Watched TV for a while; the Eurovision Song Contest was on, in German, with Polish subtitles, but I could hear Graham Norton's commentary in the background. It amused me; I chose my winners and thought about my friend David L., who, with his friends, always had a party on that night. Time for reflection; I sat in bed and thought about Warsaw and how the city had recovered from the devastation of its people and buildings, and on a far more flippant note, on how much ice cream we had eaten.

Day 21

An early start, but time enough for breakfast. My flight was earlier than that of the girls, but I saw them just before I left. Fond farewells, and then in what was to become an anthem "see you in Rock Ferry". Then it was off to the airport terminal to get my Aeroflot flight. Must say, I was a bit nervous; the thought of going on to Moscow alone was a bit daunting. I managed to get through all of the checks and on to the plane. I sat next to J., an engineer working in Russia; it was all very 'James Bondish' - well, in my imagination anyway. I had a good flight and on arrival went to the 'aliens' queue to have my papers checked. It took ages, with lots of stares, sideways glances, checks on the computer, then the whole routine repeated about three times. I started to get panicky, but finally I was through. What a relief!

I got a train to the centre to await the arrival of Collette and Kate, at the Leningradski station. Our planes had arrived within ten minutes of each other, but unfortunately at two different airports either side of Moscow. We had big hugs all around on finally meeting up, but of course, as with many things we found in Russia, not quite straight forward. The stations have many exits and we didn't meet up quite as planned, until we realised I was at the front exit and they were at the back. Also, all luggage had to go through an X-ray machine each time, a pain, but nonetheless a comforting safety procedure. So, back to the hugs; it was good to see that my next companions had arrived safely, ready for the next part of the adventure. We left our luggage at the station and went off to discover Red Square.

Hello Moscow.

Chapter 4

Collette and Kate in St. Petersburg and Moscow, Russia.

Still Day 21

I met Collette and Kate in the early 1990s when they were still at Sixth Form College. They belonged to the Glenda Jackson Youth Theatre that both of my sons were part of, a good community of talented youngsters and dedicated staff, who delighted the town (Birkenhead), with the best Musicals I have ever seen. My house became a meeting point and was alive with music, discussions and general well-being. Collette in particular stayed friendly with me over the years, so I was glad that she and her friend Kate wanted to come. Collette and I had also done the Husky Sled Charity Challenge together in 2008, and she had looked after me and my dogs in the very cold arctic wilderness.

I felt at home straight away, as we wandered around Red Square taking in the sights, the colours and the general clatter of people. We sat at an outdoor cafe and had cocktails, whilst watching the world pass by.

I find people-watching is such a fascinating thing to do, wherever I am. Our train to St. Petersburg was leaving around midnight at the Leningradski station. Collette had worked out the route there, including the names of the Metro stations, as of course they were written in the Cyrillic alphabet, and our guide map was in English. I used her no-nonsense guide to travelling around Moscow, ever after.

We enjoyed our short time at the square, but weren't too sorry to leave as we knew we were coming back. We collected our luggage, and had sandwiches and hot drinks whilst waiting for the train. The overnight trains are given a fanfare as they leave the station. We were booked onto the Red Arrow (Krasnaya Strela), the most famous of the St. Petersburg trains. Sat in the waiting area awaiting boarding to be announced.

A very busy station; once you got a seat you just didn't leave it otherwise you would end up sitting on your case. Finally the board lit up with our train number. Once on the platform, it was quite a rush looking for the carriage; Russian trains in particular do not hang around.

It was a very long train, with carriage attendants smartly dressed in their uniforms, standing by each door.

Once shown to our cabin, it was time to relax. The interior was beautifully laid out, with curtains, table laden with juices and chocolates. A touch of luxury, befitting of the train which once was the route to the old imperial capital. Time to settle for the night. Our cabin had four berths, and as there were three of us and no-one else in sight, we spread out and started to change into our nightwear.

Imagine our surprise when the door was flung open and standing there was a Russian bear of a man. I don't know who was the most taken aback, him or us. The vacant top bunk was his. Talk about awkward. He very politely stood out in the corridor whilst we finished changing and once the lights were out, came in, undressed and got into his bunk.

A word to the wise: when booking sleeper cabins, you need to specify same-sex cabins, unless you don't mind. Happened a few times during the trip, but actually it was not a problem; everyone was too tired to even talk and the movement of the train soon lulled everyone off to sleep.

Day 22

We woke up, not too bad a sleep. The breakfast packs were brought to us, and also a wash bag with toothbrush, toothpaste and so on. Bit of an upset as the man thought we had taken his wash pack and reported it to our carriage attendant, who came storming in, shouting in Russian. Once we realised what she was after, we found his pack, on his bunk. Much too early for all of that shouting. Apart from that, everything was fine; we got ready, disembarked and found a taxi to take us to our hotel, a nice, small but clean place.

We all had a rest, a shower and then went sightseeing. As with other cities, found the HoHos, did the whole route first, then second time around, got off at specific locations. The whole city was full of amazing ornate buildings, wide boulevards and imposing churches; it was not hard to imagine how grand it had once been. Having seen a number of TV dramas and films, I could almost hear the music, and see the swirling of the ball gowns; everything just shouted luxury at you, albeit somewhat faded now.

'St Petersburg is a Russian port on the Baltic Sea, in the Gulf of Finland. It was founded by Peter the Great in 1703, was the imperial capital for two centuries and remains Russia's cultural centre. Had had various names such as Petrograd in 1914, Leningrad in 1924 and back to St. Petersburg from 1991. It was the seat of the Romanov dynasty until the communist revolution of 1917. The 1905 revolution began in the city, later after the abdication of Czar Nicholas III. The Bolshevics, led by Lenin, stormed the Winter Palace. During WWII German forces besieged the city, which became the longest and most lethal siege in modern history. Elections took place in 1991 for the first mayor of the city.'

The main street is the Nevsky Prospekt, much of which was rebuilt in the classical and empire style, following the catastrophic fires which ravaged the city. Beautiful buildings such as the Marble Palace, Admiralty Building, St. Isaac's Cathedral and the Hermitage complex. Romanticist styles also dominated until 1890, evident in buildings such as the Mariinsky Palace.

One of the churches that we wanted to see was the Church of Saviour of the Spilled Blood, the spot where Czar Alexander II was assassinated in 1881. The church was closed in 1931 but later, following a 30 year restoration programme, was reopened in 1997. We were met with the sight of the most beautiful wall paintings that I certainly had ever seen.

I have never been the most religious of people, but that does not mean that I am immune to the beauty of church decoration regardless of denomination. However, I have found it difficult to reconcile the heavy gold ornamentation of some churches in the world, particularly when they were located in historically poor areas. That said, I still photographed them.

We found a small cafe, then later went to the Winter Palace and the Hermitage museum.

'The Winter Palace was the official residence of the Russian monarchs from 1732 until 1917. Designed by Bartolomeo Rastrelli, amongst others in the Elizabethan Baroque style. The interior was redesigned in various styles in 1837 following a large fire. The Palace is now a world famous museum attracting millions of visitors each year. Likewise the Hermitage, consisting of various buildings, founded by Catherine the Great in 1754, and including the largest collections of paintings in the world. Most in storage conditions but still very many on public show.'

What an amazing place. We walked through the former royal family rooms, which were as opulent as you would imagine them to be, and on into the Hermitage section.

Magnificence: gold finishings everywhere, luxury and wealth pouring from every door, ceiling, mirrored room, and that was just the building itself, never mind the treasures within it. We saw the most amazing clockwork Peacock, all gold of course, sadly not working as it was only wound up once a year but there was a video set up showing it in all of its glory. Such craftsmanship.

We spent quite some time looking at the paintings and other feasts for the eyes on show. This was another example of somewhere I had read about, and was now seeing for real. I was not disappointed.

We had our lunch in a nice little cafe at the side of the canal, where the girls were encouraged to try the 'tinctures', shots, by any other name. Well, as you can see, nearly took their heads off.

Luckily I don't drink spirits, so was saved the experience. We went back on the HoHo and out to the World Trade building and surrounding areas. You could still see the bleak grey buildings where, the KGB and other such organisations once exerted their influence, as indeed was the case in all of the old soviet countries that I visited. Again, history and reality intertwined.

Once back, we had a rest in our rooms, then at 1 a.m. we walked down to the River Neva and watched the raising of the bridges and the flotilla of boats, lit up against the dark sky.

Impressive, but you know, we all thought that the Birkenhead Four Bridges area could give it a run for its money. Time to go back for bed.

Day 23

A leisurely start to the day. We went sightseeing again, but this time by boat, along the river and past the Summer Palace, now also a museum, but originally completed in 1714 as a residence for Peter the Great and his family. We also saw the Battlecruiser Aurora, the ship that had, according to legend, in 1917, fired the first shot at the Winter Palace, signalling the start of the October Revolution.

We had our lunch in a quirky little place called "The Idiots Cafe", a nod to the works of writer Dostoevsky. A bohemian atmosphere, with good food too. Later we went across the main bridge to the Peter and Paul Fortress and Cathedral. These buildings occupy a dominant position on the right bank of the River Neva, on Zayachy Island.

Each noon a blank cannon shot is fired to mark the time. It had started to rain, and we learnt that in Russia they don't just have rainfall; oh no, it came down in absolute torrents, so to say we were a bit wet when we arrived there was an understatement. That, coupled with the fact that although it looked a short distance away, it was in reality a long walk.

Sadly most of the fortress was closed, but we did manage to see the Cathedral and the tombs of the Romanovs.

We also went to the prison, where Collette went to a higher floor to view the cells, leaving Kate and I to await her return. She was gone for a long time and arrived back looking harassed and unsettled, very unlike her. Seems there was a one-way system and the guards would not let her back down the stairs. We couldn't hear her, so she had to go out of the building, then re-enter. Of course, she did not then have a ticket, but was finally able to convince someone that she did not want to break into the prison, but to break Kate and me out.

We all needed a drink after that, so found a restaurant/bar to unwind, and await a taxi, the rain still incredibly heavy. When it finally arrived, the poor driver had spent over half an hour getting over the bridge; there was so much traffic, we should have walked, we were wet anyway. The lady driver was very gracious about the whole thing, thankfully. Back at our rooms, we got changed and went out to a Georgian restaurant, Rustica, and had the best food I have had so far. Even the rain had the grace to stop.

We collected our luggage and went on to the station for the overnight train back to Moscow. We met an eccentric English lady travelling through Europe, but only going as far as Russia. She and I chatted about routes and experiences so far. We boarded the overnight express; it was not as grand as the Red Arrow, but it had a friendlier atmosphere. Again we thought we had the cabin to ourselves, especially as the train had already left the station before the fourth passenger appeared. Thankfully a very nice Russian lady, Olga. We chatted for a while, (as long as you do not discuss anything controversial, everything is fine), then slept. Not a bad journey at all.

Day 24

We arrived back in Moscow, and went straight to the Yannu 1905 district where we had hired the flat.

We went on the Metro, such an efficient system with trains every two minutes. I had a bit of a scare on the escalator, tripped over my case and lost balance. Fortunately the girls caught me and Collette took charge. There were a few tears; I put it down to tiredness as I had already travelled through five countries. Came out of the station to be met with the sight of a very large sculpture.

This had been commissioned to commemorate the Revolution of 1905, when a wave of political and social unrest swept through vast areas of the Empire. This was made up of peasant protests, workers strikes and military mutinies. It did have some effect though, as it led to the Russian Constitution of 1906, multiparty system, many reforms and the eventual establishment of the State Duma.

I phoned Danil, the owner of the flat, who came to meet us. A really nice, funny guy; we all liked him immediately. The flat was within five minutes walk from the Metro. It was in a typically austere building, as you would expect to see in Russia, but the flat itself was a good size, comfortable and welcoming. I was there seven days overall and felt very safe and actually quite at home. Once we had settled our things in, I decided to stay there whilst the girls went out exploring. I was not inactive; I spent my time doing two loads of washing and wandering down to the supermarket, taking in the local scenery as I went. It was so hot, I hadn't expected that. I was glad that the girls had some time to themselves, especially as they were younger and able to move about so much quicker. Besides I was going to be there longer than them. Once they were back, and after a rest, we all went to a restaurant conveniently situated at the corner of the block. Good food too. We swapped stories before bed, theirs slightly more interesting than mine. They had been inside the Kremlin complex which hands down beats a supermarket shop any day. I fell into a welcome sleep.

Day 25 May 15th

Made ourselves a leisurely breakfast, then we went off to join the free walking tour we had found on-line. The guide was a lovely girl called Elena who spoke excellent English and was very knowledgeable. Our group were all English speakers, but from lots of different countries. It was fascinating listening to everyone's stories. There was a lot to see, and learn about. She was a very funny girl who told us jokes, harmless enough but even so, I'm sure they would not have been allowed until the recent past. I learnt about things I did not know and she even managed to change some of my misconceptions in regard to Russia.

She was a very good ambassador for her country, steering away from subjects that were not up for discussion, and the group honoured that. The route took us to churches, Romanov houses, Red Square, Lenin's tomb and the changing of the Guards at the tomb of the Unknown Warrior. It was all fascinating.

We went inside the large RYM departmental store, and had ice creams sitting by the fountain.

Apparently, so the story goes, if it is said anywhere in Russia "I'll meet you by the fountain", everyone would know that it was at the one in the departmental store on Red Square. An amazing complex built in 1893. Another story was that during the 1950s there was a plan to knock it down and rebuild it with a Soviet style building but legend has it that a revolt by the Kremlin wives stopped that, as it was the only place where many items could be bought. People would come from all over Russia to buy things, sometimes travelling from places like Siberia, maybe just to buy kitchen items, a two week round trip.

After lunch we went to a women's Bath House; now that was an experience.

I opted out of the steam room, far too hot, so spent the time in a small pool getting more wrinkly by the minute, waiting for the girls. We all came out a little bemused, especially as the naked female attendants, a little reminiscent of the old style shot putters/all-in wrestlers, were determined the girls were going to have the steam room and sauna experience whether they wanted to or not! Still it added to the memories, and stories, to bring home with us.

Collette and Kate were flying home later that evening, so we just had time for dinner, collect their luggage and then off they went. As there were two of them, I did not go to the airport, but said our goodbyes at the flat. As with my other friends, I was sorry to see them go; I had enjoyed our time together. I spent a quiet evening watching TV, Hawaii 5 0, in Russian, and later standing out on the small balcony watching the traffic and looking at the lights of central Moscow. The flat had a series of doors to lock, so I felt very safe as I went to bed.

Chapter 5

Jo in Moscow

Jo is my friend and colleague whom I first met when she came to work at the Blood Transfusion Service. I liked her straight away, and felt that I had met a kindred spirit. A lady with a large family, who all welcomed me into their fold. I am so happy that she chose to be part of this adventure.

Day 26

I awoke to a text saying that the girls were safely home. I pottered around and then decided that I would go into the centre. As I was going to be three days on my own, I didn't want to become a prisoner of my own making in the flat. It got to 12 noon, and I was still dithering about, so I gave myself a good talking to and went out. I felt quite vulnerable as I left the sanctuary of the flat, but once outside all was fine. I went along to the Metro station, photographed the statue I mentioned, then got on to the train to the centre, and got off at Red Square. So far so good. I walked down towards the

Kremlin and past the Lubyanka, formally a KGB Prison and Interrogation centre. Now there, I was sure, was a building with many stories to tell. I had been surprised at how much I liked it here; there was so much to see and do and I had discovered it really was no problem being on my own.

I went to find the HoHo bus stop. The tickets came with three options, Bus Tour, River Cruise and Bus and Boat Tour. I chose the Bus Tour, and followed the Red Route first as it seemed appropriate. I listened to the commentary and learnt more about the buildings, history and such like. The bus went down to the terminal where the Red and Green Routes met up. This was beside a small park and the canal. A traditional place where newly-weds came for photo sessions and also placed their 'love locks' on the purpose-built metal trees.

There were so many beautiful and interesting buildings, which included the 'Seven Sisters'. These were the skyscrapers that defined the skyline of Moscow.

They were built during the Stalinist era for the glorification of the Soviet State, after WWII, to rival American buildings in design and height. Each building was adorned with Soviet logos.

A red star was currently the latest emblem, not on the buildings but as sculptures present in prominent areas.

Occasionally the double headed eagle, the symbol of Imperial Russia could be seen.

An eighth 'sister' was due to be built, but as yet the designated area in central Moscow still lay empty.

I saw the Cathedral of Christ the Savior, a Russian Orthodox Church which has the reputation of being the tallest Orthodox Christian Church in the World. It has an interesting past; built originally in the 19th century, it was destroyed in 1931 to make way for the building of the Palace of the

Soviets. Legend had it that the Abbess laid a curse, that any building ever built there, would not last more than 50 years. The 'Palace' was never built due to WWII and lack of funds. In Khrushchev's time it became the world's largest open air swimming pool. However, in 1990 permission was given for the rebuilding of the Cathedral in its original form and by 2000 the work was completed. In 2012 members of a certain female rock band were arrested there for expressing political and irreligious opinions.

I arrived back around 6 p.m., got a take-away and went home to the flat. It had been a most enjoyable day, a real treat for all of the senses. More than I could say for the TV, but then, you can't have everything.

Day 27

Roused myself earlier today. Once I had realised that I was okay to wander around on my own, I got more adventurous and was looking forward to another day of exploration. This time, the first step was the Alexander Gardens, just outside The Kremlin walls. The gardens were beautifully laid out, and housed the most amazing large fountain called 'The Seasons of the Year', that incorporated four larger than life horses that reared up in the spray. There were a lot of people there, most of whom were Russian.

I also went also to the Lenin Mausoleum, queued up and went inside. A strange place, with Lenin's open coffin in the middle, looking quite like a Madame Tussaud waxwork figure. No photographs were allowed, and there were many guards there to enforce that. I touched the walls, pretending to overbalance. Later I walked alongside the Kremlin walls where there were many other graves and plaques of other notable citizens such as Gagarin, Stalin, Zhukov, Sverdlov, Andropov, Kalanin and Brezhnev amongst others.

I saw in passing the Bolshoi Ballet building, but sadly I hadn't been organised enough to get a ticket for any of the performances, maybe next time.

I got another HoHo to the canal area and really liked it there. I must show it to Jo and Vicky. I was lucky to see an unusual rainbow.

I later tried to find the Gulag Museum but no joy, so I returned to the flat and made ready for Jo's arrival. It felt strange in some ways, but also very natural to be making up beds and going to the supermarket, but instead of home, it was a flat in Moscow, where I must say I felt equally at home.

It soon became time to go, so following Collette's excellent instructions I went off on the Metro, then on an overland bus to the airport. It was lovely to see a tired, but excited Jo arriving. After lots of hugs we set off back to the flat. I managed to get us there with only one slight miscalculation that was easily rectified. I have to say that of all the places I have been, the Moscow Metro is without equal. It was not just the ornate stations with their statues and art works, but the frequency of the trains; you never had to run for one as the next one followed within two minutes. Also, as I am an older lady, I was, on every occasion, offered a seat. I was very impressed.

We went back to the flat, cup of tea for me, coffee for Jo, unpacked, had a rest and an unwinding session to allow Jo to settle in.

It had been very hot. I hadn't expected such high temperatures as Moscow always sounded cold somehow, so we enjoyed relaxing in the coolness of the flat. We later went around the corner for our evening meal and then, after a good natter, we settled down for an exhausted but happy sleep.

Day 28

I received a text to say that my niece had given birth to a baby boy, to be called Ben. Life just goes on, whether you are there or not, but you do not always feel that far away because of all of the available technology. We had a leisurely breakfast and then made a plan for the day. First stop was to be the RYM store for an ice cream; well, Jo needed to have that experience too, and a look around Red Square whilst we were there.

'The square, originally a slum outside of the fortress walls, was cleared on the orders of Ivan III in the 1400s. The name derives from the word 'krasnyi' which originally meant 'beautiful', but has had various names during its history, such as Trinity Square and Fire Square. During the 20th Century it was famous as the site of ostentatious military parades showcasing the equipment and might of the Soviet Armed Forces. Latterly, following Perestroika, the area has been used for different events such as classical Music Concerts, Rock Concerts, Circuses and generally as a tourist location.'

The walls of the Kremlin could be seen along one side of the square. There are many Kremlins throughout Russia, but the main, and best known is the Moscow Kremlin. It is a fortified complex in the heart of the city. The site had been continuously inhabited since 2BC, with the word Kremlin first recorded in 1331. The fortress had been occupied by many of the Tsars, including Peter the Great, until he moved his capital to

St. Petersburg, then later by Catherine the Great and Nicholas I amongst others. It had also been the residence of Lenin and later Stalin in the Soviet era. The complex contains many beautiful buildings, including four Cathedrals, five Palaces and the tomb of Ivan the Terrible. It now housed the official residence of the President of the Russian Federation.

We decided to walk down to St. Basil's Basilica.

Its real name was the Cathedral of Vassily the Blessed, built on the orders of Ivan the Terrible in 1555–1561. It is said that Ivan blinded the Architects on completion of the building, so that it could not be replicated. Amazing architecture, but considering the size of the building, the inside felt very small, as each domed area, being an individual church, had limited floor space. It was like nothing I had ever experienced before. We were both impressed.

We went on to see the Changing of the Guards ceremony, carried out with much precision, every hour on the hour.

It was so hot, those poor soldiers must have been melting. Speaking of soldiers, we saw many uniformed men and women, not all were military, some were police, guards, hotel doormen, delivery people, but all very smart in their appearance. They were just part of the tapestry of the city.

From there we meandered around Alexander Gardens, and played in the waters surrounding the large horse fountain. Running the gauntlet of the lines of water spouts, we laughed and shouted like happy children. We studied the other statues dotted around the area, mostly depictions from Fairy Tales.

We, of course, managed to fit in eating in various places, but the food came second compared to the bounty before our eyes.

We found the HoHo bus and travelled down to Bolotnaya Square, the terminal by the canal. We went to see a large sculpture in the small park.

The sculpture, called 'Children are the Victims of Adult Vices' by M. Chemiakin, was intended to be an allegory of the fight against global evil, a call to action to save the living and future generations. The semicircle of figures were meant to represent the Golden Children (the innocents), Drug Addiction, Prostitution, Theft, Alcoholism, Ignorance, Irresponsible Science, Indifference, Violence, Sadism, Those without Memory, Child Labour, Poverty and War. It was very thought provoking.

We decided to go on a cruise along the Canal, to the Peter I monument. The story went that the monument was originally made to depict Christopher Columbus, but no city wanted to buy it, so it was resculpted as Peter and given to Moscow. We travelled along the River Moskva which gave us magnificent views of the Kremlin outer walls and the churches within. The churches all around the city were very striking with their colourful onion shaped domes. I felt very relaxed and quite sleepy.

We returned to the square in time for souvenir shopping at the stalls set up there, then it was back to the flat to make final preparations for our trip on the TransSiberian/Mongolian train to Beijing.

Danil's friend arrived to receive the keys from us, and phoned for a taxi. We had far too much luggage for the Metro, but on reflection we should have made the effort. The taxi driver seemed nice enough, friendly and helpful until I noticed that he had changed the route on his Sat Nav a number of times, and also that we had gone up the same road twice. I mentioned it and he pretended not to understand. After a good five minutes of this nonsense I decided to take charge. Even though we did have enough time to get to the train, I started to get anxious about missing it, and before long I went into a full blown panic attack.

Unfortunately I couldn't really warn Jo, who became really worried. The driver by now was having a minor panic of his own, thinking he had a very ill foreigner in his taxi. I managed to wink at Jo and to make doubly sure that she was aware of my subterfuge, I wrote on a post card that was in my handbag, 'GOOD ACTRESS'.

Suddenly, we were back on route and arrived at the Yaroslavsky station very quickly. The driver was out of the taxi before you could look around, shouting "where train, where train?" The luggage was out of the boot and off he ran leaving the boot open. He took my luggage; Jo had her own, we both had a wry smile. I kept up my 'attack' until he had gone, then we both had a good laugh. I hated getting ripped off. It was not so much the money, it was the assumption that tourists are stupid and don't know what was going on. To be fair, the majority of people we met in Russia were extremely helpful, friendly and made us feel very welcomed and part of the city.

And so, to the train. Jo and I were so excited. There were a number of people waiting on the platform looking expectantly for the train. There were Chinese families, some Europeans from who knows where, and of course, us. Once the train arrived we had to wait for the cleaning cycle to be done, so we spent our time taking photos and saying goodbye to Moscow, although in my case I would be coming back with Vicky.

Chapter 6

TransSiberian Train – outwards

'The TransSiberian Railway is a network of railways connecting Moscow with the east of Russia. It is the longest railway line in the world with branch lines into Mongolia, China and North Korea. It connects the European and Asian sections of Russia. Built between 1891 and 1916 under the supervision of Government Ministers appointed by Tsar Alexander III and Tsar Nicholas II. The track between Moscow and Vladivostok takes eight days and runs through eight time zones and stretches for 5,772 miles.

'The line through to Mongolia branches off at Ulan-Ude, passing Ulan Bataar and on to Beijing. After the Russian Revolution of 1917 the railway became a vital communications link, the line mainly used by Russian citizens and increasingly more tourists. The journey starts at the Moscow Yaroslavsky Rail Terminal. The TransManchurian section branches off at Chita, then on to Beijing. The BAM junction (Baikal – Amur Mainline), diverts from the TransSiberian at Tayshet, and was built as an alternative to that line, especially along the sections that border China. The lines are also used by Goods trains carrying freight to Europe.'

Still Day 28

At last, it was time for Jo and me to be escorted to our Cabin. When the door was opened, I initially experienced some disappointment. I suppose I thought it would be like the Krasnaya Strela to St. Petersburg, all fancy curtains and table cloths, but it was rather bare and utilitarian looking. The trains were either Russian or Chinese, ours being Chinese. I said nothing because Jo was so happy, so I wasn't going to dampen her enthusiasm. We did however have a sink/shower type space that we shared with the next door cabin with a series of interlocking doors. The toilet was at the end of our short corridor. Our carriage contained eight cabins, and also the small office and living quarters of the guard.

The feeling was short-lived once we were in and started to put our things in place. We hung up our clothes, put the food into the lockers under the seats, made up our beds and set our table with nibbles, drinks, quiz books and cameras. It very quickly became our 'home', and of course the little bathroom was a wonderful addition.

Shame on me for having had such negative thoughts. Just time for a midnight feast, jammies on and bed, as the train slid, not so silently, out of the station. We left the curtains open for a while, and watched the stars that were so close that you felt you could just pluck them out of the sky.

Day 29 May 21st

The first stop was Vladimir, located on the Klyazma River.

This was one of the medieval capitals of Russia, founded around 1108, until it was superseded by Moscow as the site of the crowning of the Grand Princes. It was overrun by Mongol–Tartar hordes and never really recovered its position. A city of beautiful white stone buildings.

I had a pretty disturbed night, but then I never sleep well at the best of times. I was sure it would get better, especially with the rocking of the train. We had to get used to the noise too, but in a strange way it was comforting, the clattering of the wheels on the tracks made different sounds depending on the speed. We had our own train symphony.

We woke up to see the dawn, and took photos of course. The train was just travelling past forests and the odd town. We stopped at Nizhny

Novograd, called Gorky, in reference to Alexei Maximovich Peskov, writer and founder of the Socialist Realism Literary Method and a political activist, five times Nobel Prize nominee, who died in 1936.

We were still on Moscow time, but this would change as we travelled across the vast expanse that is Russia. Had a breakfast of instant porridge, bread, jam and tea. We used the boiling water from the samovar at the end of the corridor; it was great to have hot water available at all times.

We spent time looking out of the window at the scenery rushing by, also took lots of photos, most of which were unusable. You would not believe how many pylons, telegraph poles, trees and of course the ultra long goods trains that would obscure the views.

Funny thing was, that you never noticed them as you lined your shot up, but without fail, there they were. It got to be a standing joke from there onwards.

Jo consulted her travel book and was able to tell us what to expect at each kilometre; it was a great help and fun too. We saw the Volga River, then came to a very built up area, name of Perm. The city was located on the banks of the Kama River and was first mentioned in 1647 and later came the emergence of the modern city after development by Peter the Great. In the 1930s the city grew mainly because of its munitions factories and now had the largest industrial output of all cities in the Urals.

We went to the restaurant car for lunch. The meal looked tiny but was surprisingly filling. We spent the afternoon doing crosswords from our puzzle books. I later had a nap, then we played cards and generally spent the time chatting and peering out of the window. I tried to take more photos. In the evening, after our meal, the first of many that involved Pot Noodles, we waited to see the Europe/Asia border, marked by a large obelisk at the side of the track.

Later into the night, whilst star gazing from the corridor window, the train stopped suddenly and everyone was thrown about the carriages. Our guard, a very pleasant Chinese guy, told us that he thought someone or something had been hit, by making the universal sign of cutting the throat. We understood. We were stopped for quite some time whilst the railmen looked under the train with their torches. Eventually we were underway, not really knowing the outcome of the delay.

The next stop was Ykaterinburg, known as Sverdlovsk in the Soviet era, the main industrial and cultural centre of the region. Founded in 1723 and named after the lady who eventually became Catherine I. The city was an important transit route following the October Revolution, and was the location where Tsar Nicholas II and his family were imprisoned in the Ipatiev House then later executed on July 17th 1918.

A city with a very varied past, its surrounding area was also the location of the U-2 Spy plane incident in 1960 when American Francis Gary Powers was shot down and later exchanged in East Berlin for the KGB spy Rudolf Abel. I remember the incident happening and have also been to the very bridge where the exchange took place, but that as they say, is another story.

I finally went to sleep, but as usual, I was up to greet the dawn.

Day 30

We watched as the sun came up and shone through the thickly wooded areas of Silver Birch.

Jo told me a story about her family connections and recollections in regard to the Birch trees. The train stopped at Omsk so I hopped off to get some supplies. Talk about a disgrace; I was still in my pyjamas, hair unbrushed and teeth uncleaned. Dear, dear me. Felt like I was in a scene from my home town, although to be fair the young girls there did at least have on some make-up. Strange fashion, going to town in your pyjamas. I got the supplies, bread, some cheese, apples and milk.

We had a nice breakfast. It was 1 p.m., and I finally went to get washed, lazy item. Jo too; talk about a relaxed morning. This was the great advantage of having a shared wash room and a private cabin.

The train was due to go through the Steppes next. Cameras at the ready. The river Om was in the distance. We came into Ob, then travelled over a large bridge with seven spans that crossed the river.

We had our next stop at Barabinsk, where there were lots of platform hawkers, some even selling Fish.

I had my afternoon nap, then spent hours staring out of the window at the ever changing scenery.

The train did not travel very quickly so there was time to see things and, with a bit of luck, photograph them, UNLESS it was something of great importance. Then the train flew past in a great spurt of speed and a long goods train would jump into view just in time to totally obscure the chance of any reasonable photograph, amazing.

Had our tea meal. Must say with what Jo brought out from England, plus my Moscow supermarket shop, and what we bought on the platforms, we did ourselves proud, soup and a roll, pot noodles, biscuits and hot chocolate. Later on we watched Spring Kitchen and Bees in Northampton courtesy of Jo's TV on her Tablet. We watched the night sky for a while then settled down for a sleep.

Unfortunately after the lovely day we had, there was no rest at all; the train rocked and rolled all night. It felt more like being on a stormy sea, and our symphony had become a cacophony.

Day 31

We have reached the half-way point, from Moscow to Beijing. I upped my energy levels with porridge for breakfast, had a shower and put on all clean clothes. I felt much better, camera finger twitching already. At Ilanslaya, we saw many more food sellers on the platform.

We travelled past rivers, logging areas, the occasional logging camp and general scenes of daily life.

We came to the junction of the BAM which veered off as we continued on our way. There were still lots to see and photograph, and we also decided to take photos of the goods trains, strategically placed to obliterate everything else, so if you can't beat them... I had my nap, which became a bit of a ritual, then we thought that we might explore the train. Considering that we had nowhere else to go, our days had become filled and felt quite busy. On the bends we watched our train from the window snaking through the countryside.

Remember the milk I had bought from the station? It turned out to be condensed milk, affectionately known as connie-onnie, so that was now in our tea. It reminded me of growing up at my parent's house as that was how the tea was made, although in adulthood I switched to cow's milk. We had just passed point km 4672, the Sayan Range, which was the frontier between Siberia and Mongolia. The most amazing sunset was taking place, such beautiful colours, we watched from both sides of the train for hours. We had our evening meal, played cards, taught each other games that we knew, relaxed and made ready for bed.

Day 32

I woke up with the train slowing down, looked out and it saw it was still dark. We had pulled into Irkurst. New passengers were getting on. I tried to take photos but they were not good, so I went back to sleep for a while. Our next place of visual note was Lake Baikal where we arrived at 4 a.m.

'This is a massive ancient lake, said to be the world's deepest, with crystal clear water and unique wildlife, thought to be home to more than 2000 species of plants and animals, with 60% being found nowhere else. It has been designated a UNESCO World Heritage site. It is 636 kms long, and 81 kms wide, and estimated to be about 25 million years old.'

I woke Jo as requested. We got our cameras ready, and we were not disappointed. What magnificent views, an absolutely huge area with mountains bordering the shoreline. We stayed awake whilst we travelled past fishing villages, a large industrial town area and isolated farmsteads.

Finally tiredness overtook us so we went back to sleep and awoke three hours later to find that we were still travelling around the lake.

We had some food, got dressed and spent the time sightseeing from the comfort of our cabin as the train moved on through Ulan-Ude, the junction of the Trans-Mongolian Railway, and on to the Mongolian border. We arrived at the border crossing, where the guards and customs staff came through the train, checking cabins, passports, well everything really. It took three hours at the Russian side and a similar amount of time at the Mongolian end. Then finally we were on our way to Ulan Bataar.

Something to keep in mind, the toilets were locked for at least 15 minutes each side of arriving at and departing from a station, and of course, the time spent at the stop itself. This also applied for any type of stop, border checks, wheel changing and so on. We soon learnt to take that into account.

Day 33 Mongolia

'Located in the Tuul river valley, bordering the Bogd Khan Uul National Park, Ulan Bataar is the capital of Mongolia. A famous son was Temujin, later known as Genghis Khan who was the founder of the Mongol Empire. In 1639 a Buddhist monastic centre was in existence and remained a mobile monastery town until it settled into its permanent location in 1778. In 1924 the town came under the control of Soviet Russia and named Ulanbataar meaning Red Hero. The Trans-Mongolian railway was completed in 1956, and urban planning began and the city as it now is, emerged. Although there is still evidence of soviet style architecture, many buildings have been upgraded and modified to allow for small shops on

the ground floors. The city now boasts cinemas, several large departmental stores and museums.'

Mongolia's capital took us by surprise in a number of ways. We arrived around 6 a.m., the train shuddered to a halt, then it was a rush job getting on enough clothes so that we could get off. To be honest it was a case of things on over our pyjamas. The train never stayed anywhere very long, although we had a little more time than usual whilst the Mongolian restaurant car was attached.

There were a lot of people milling about on the station, so we joined the melee. An eye had to be kept on the train because there was no warning that it was about to leave, no announcements, whistles from the guards or the train itself. We couldn't leave the station, not just due to the time factor, but also we only had transit visas. We had wanted to stay for a few days, but were advised that it would be difficult to get another cabin for the remainder of the journey to Beijing. Reluctantly we decided to complete the trip in one section.

What we saw from the station was a bit disappointing as it looked to be a jumbly city of 60s style skyscrapers and neon signs.

Not exactly what we had expected, although I am sure outside the city limits it would have been very different. We re-boarded the train, had our breakfast. One thing about having your own food, you can eat whenever you like, and we did ourselves proud, washed down with a cup or two of tea.

Once we had left the station the scenery became much more interesting. The outskirts showed that people still lived the traditional way, although with modern twists, such as yurts with big cars/trucks parked outside.

We saw small holdings, cattle being rounded up by motorbike and large numbers of horses and camels grazing.

We loved the contrast as compared to everything else we had seen. At km573 it was the start of the Gobi desert. I couldn't believe it; here was some magical place in the East that I had learnt about at school, and now I was seeing it with my own eyes. We saw large swathes of sand and scrubland, and on the horizon, a huge statue rising up out of the ground.

We also saw the Zaisan Memorial sculpture depicting scenes of friendship between Russia and Mongolia.

A quote from Jo: "We saw yurts, ponies, camels, sand, grasses, little yellow flowers, birds of prey and people; awe inspiring indeed".

Later we came into a small town, name of Choyr, where we saw an astronaut and an angel. Well, definitely the astronaut, Juderdemidiin Gurragchaa, who was the first Mongolian in space. He was an aerospace engineer and took part in the 1981 Soyuz 39 mission that docked with Salyut 6 where he spent seven days in space.

Of course, it was his commemorative statue that we saw, pointing towards the heavens.

The angel? That was an old piece of pipe that stuck up out of the ground at the side of the track. I saw an angel immediately, took a photo and spent the next hour showing it to Jo, from all angles, and tried to convince her that it was our guardian angel. I was sure of it; she however was having none of it, and I suppose she could have been right to have just the tiniest doubt about my sanity. I shall print the photo and rest my case.

We were able to get off the train at the next stop, so I wandered off taking photographs whist Jo found a vendor selling paintings.

He was actually the artist and was there with his son. He spoke some English and asked us where we were from. We said Birkenhead, but were met with blank stares, so we said near Liverpool for clarification. "Oh" he said, "football" and then coyly said "me, Manchester United". So there we were, in the middle of nowhere, having a conversation about football. Well you would, wouldn't you? We bought some of his smaller paintings depicting nomadic life, then said goodbye to him and his son. He was a really nice friendly guy, a pleasure to talk with, and a good artist too.

Back on the train we decided to go to the restaurant car that had been attached at the border, in place of the Russian one. Interesting décor, but the food sadly didn't compare. Still, food was food and a change from pot noodles.

I went back to taking more photos like a woman possessed. I went through them each night to delete the failures, and there were many of those. The Gobi desert was amazing; we just loved it, the vast emptiness of it gave it a unique beauty. Merely the thought of where this was, and the occasional glimpses of life were fascinating and made the whole experience one to be treasured.

We arrived at the Mongolian border station and had to give in our Passports. All very official. As we left we could see that soldiers were saluting the train. We travelled a relatively short distance to Erlian station for the Chinese border stop. Jo and I had decided to take a 'selfie' but we were quite inept at such things; you know, angles all wrong, too close, not ready and so on, so consequently we were some time messing about and laughing like schoolgirls. We finally we managed a shot, but unbeknownst to us, it was our turn for inspection, and there waiting patiently in the doorway was a border guard, so consequently she was in our photo too. Luckily for us she was good humoured.

Day 34

It was just past midnight, and so technically the next day. Music played us into the station, a greeting that came out of the dark night. An announcement was made giving us the option to get off the train and go to the cafe area, or to stay on it whilst it was taken away, carriage by carriage to the sheds where the wheel bogies were changed. The rail gauge in China was different to that of Russia or Mongolia.

    Jo and I opted to stay on the train, partly to see what happened but we also felt that if we got tired, we could settle down on our bunks. The train sheds were fascinating; each carriage was shunted into position by an old work-horse of an engine. Large hydraulic jacks either side of the tracks lifted the carriages up, one by one, then once the wheels were exposed they were detached and new ones fitted. I had never experienced anything like before. A first. As each carriage was done, the shunting engine moved it outside to the main track where it was re-attached to the original engine. Gradually everything was back in place, and it was time to move onwards to Beijing. The whole operation took about three hours. As we left the station we could see armed soldiers, camouflaged by strategically placed trees. The music played on.

We slept then, and awoke to very different scenery. We were now travelling through China. Lovely views, small farmsteads, people out tilling the fields. We had been told that the Great Wall could be seen from the train, running along the tops of the hills. I thought I had glimpsed it at one point, but I wasn't too worried about capturing it on camera, as a visit to the wall itself was on our itinerary.

We started to pack up our belongings, food and souvenirs ready to disembark at Beijing station. We felt sad; this little cabin had been our home for six days and we had enjoyed our time in it; the great conversations, visits to the restaurant cars, our own food preparation. Also the many cups of tea and coffee thanks to the efforts of our guard, constantly stoking the fire under the samovar for our supply of hot water and of course the ever changing scenery as we went through the different time zones. If that was Siberia, well, we loved it. Of course it was summer, and we realised that it would have been very different for the prisoners of the past.

Our favourite section, we both agreed, was Mongolia, travelling across the edge of the desert, riding the tracks in and out of history.

Once we were packed, we sat back and watched as the landscape became more and more urbanised, and mentally prepared ourselves for the next phase of our adventure.

Chapter 7

Beijing, China

Still Day 34

Then suddenly, here we were, Beijing.

We went outside and the extreme heat hit us, well that and the constant hassling by street hawkers and taxi drivers. Much more about them later. I had previously been told where to queue for a taxi, gave the driver instructions provided by our hosts, and set off to find the courtyard house in the Hutong districts of Dongchen. What a joy, the place was amazing.

Coffee, one of the owners, was waiting for us in the alley as the taxi pulled up. We had given the driver my phone, who spoke to her to get more detailed instructions, a trick we could have done within our subsequent dealings, mostly disastrous, with taxi drivers. She was a lovely, happy person who gave us a very warm welcome. We absolutely loved the little house, and felt right at home immediately. Coffee showed us where everything was, then left us to settle in. There was everything we needed; a well stocked kitchen, bedroom each, lounge area with TV/DVD and an interconnecting bathroom between each bedroom. Excellent use of a very small space. The courtyard in the middle, was open to the stars, and there was a high wall and very sturdy door out to the alley. Everything could be individually locked so we felt very safe.

We had something to eat and a rest, then in the evening went out for a walk in the neighbourhood.

Lights, food smells, lots of people, some were even dancing in a local park. Loved it. We just stood and soaked up the atmosphere. We learnt that the Hutongs were Beijing's traditional alleyways, originally the centre of the old neighbourhoods, mostly courtyard houses, in and around the Forbidden City. We were delighted to be staying in such an amazing area steeped in history.

We went to a small local supermarket for some supplies, then back in our new home, a cup of tea, and where better to have such a drink than in the home of the Tea Ceremonies, followed by an earlyish night. We were both so overcome with the adventures and experiences of the day.

Day 35

Oh dear, it was 02.30 and I was awake, and it was already very hot. Mustn't wake Jo, although this would be unlikely as her room was across the courtyard. I eventually went back to sleep. Once up, had breakfast we got ready in a very leisurely way.

We had decided to go and see the Forbidden City. Our house was very close to the walls of the city, but not, unfortunately, near to the doorway leading in, so we had a fair walk. However, this is not a complaint; we were in a fantastic location and the walk enabled us to see the local area. The Dongchen area was very busy with people going about their normal business. Lots of smells, colours, chatter and people everywhere. We both liked it and felt at ease.

We found the entrance and emerged into a large open square in front of the main gates. There we met Michael, an English speaking guide, who persuaded us to hire him for a walking tour. We were unsure at first, but it sounded a good deal, so we bought our entrance tickets and off we went. Well, it was a very good deal; he was an excellent guide and a nice person too. He allowed for the fact that I was older and slower, so he fitted in a number of shaded resting places. He was very knowledgeable and explained what each building was, it's function and even what the roof decorations signified.

'The Purple Forbidden City, as it was known from its Chinese translation of Zijin Cheng, now just known as the Forbidden City. Constructed from 1406 to 1420, with the labours of over a million workers, it covers 170 acres and has over 180 buildings, made up of an Inner and Outer Court. Was the Chinese Imperial Palace, from the Ming Dynasty until the end of the Qing Dynasty, overall the home of 24 Emperors until the abdication of Puyi in 1912, when it ceased to be the centre of political power. The City is surrounded by a 26' high wall which acts in both a defensive and

containment function. At the southern end is the Meridian Gate, and at the northern end, the Gate of Divine Might.'

The Outer Court is made of various Halls, such as the Hall of Supreme Harmony, used for affairs of state and such functions. The Hall of Central Harmony where the Emperor would rest before and during ceremonies and the Hall of Preserving Harmony which was used for rehearsing ceremonies.

The Inner Court was also made up of 3 Halls, the Hall of Heavenly Purity, the Hall of Union and the Palace of Earthly Tranquillity. They were the official residences of the Emperor (representing Yang) and Empress (Yin). The two would meet in the Hall of Union where they would mix to produce Harmony. There were many other Halls and Residences of the family and their retainers, and the whole amazing location had gardens and a park as part of the complex. It was made a World Heritage Site in 1987, and was still undergoing a restoration programme to restore it to its original pre - 1912 state. The whole place absolutely needs to be seen to be believed.

So much history. We even learnt about the lion guardian statues and their various roles. We were just amazed at all of the architecture. Took loads of photographs. After looking at various buildings, we went to a beautiful garden that had been the private area for the wives and children to spend time in. So peaceful and beautifully laid out.

We came to some large doors leading out to the road. I gave him the agreed money which he promptly gave back, because, he said, the tour was not finished yet. The garden continued over the other side of the road, which had been built in modern times to help with Beijing's traffic problems. We were both very impressed with his honesty and fairness; we would not have known where the tour ended.

The garden gave way to Jing Shan park and woodland. We saw the area where the Chongzhen Emperor had committed suicide by hanging himself from a tree in 1644 after his city fell to rebel forces. A stone monument marked the place. Michael then took us to a Tea Room where we took part in a Tea Ceremony.

This ceremony was known in various Asian cultures, having first taken place in China. Used originally in Monasteries for herbal medicine procedures. Traditional Tea Ceremonies were known as He Jing Yi Zhen meaning peace, quiet, enjoyment and truth, and was thought to blend together the philosophies of Buddhism, Taoism and Confucianism. Benefits began to be seen for traditional gatherings, cultural and social.

Apparently various aspects had to be taken into consideration during the ceremony, such as the Tea selection, pure water, it should be relaxed, in a clean, comfortable ambient atmosphere, and the serving should be graceful with traditional clothing, using beautiful china teapots, cups and a brewing tray. Our ceremony had all of this. One of the loveliest things I had ever participated in; Jo and I really enjoyed the experience.

Once outside we went to a room where a very nice old gentleman, purportedly the great nephew of the last Emperor, made calligraphy scrolls.

I had one done for Simon and Penny for 'double happiness', complete with their names. Jo should have paid more for a bigger scroll with all of the names of her big family, but he was impressed by her and very kindly put all of the names on and charged her the same price. The finished items were really beautiful. After finally paying and thanking Michael, we walked back to a main gate, stopping to watch people dancing, just for the pure joy of it.

Then home around the outside of the city walls. People watching all of the way.

We got home exhausted but happy. Tea meal, telly and bed.

Day 36

Had a better night's sleep. 06.30 and I was awake, listening to the birds singing. We have a good day planned, I think. We had a card from Michael with his agency's number, so we booked a car with a driver and another English-speaking guide. We went to the pick-up point and a large air-conditioned car pulled up, with plenty of room inside, a nice friendly driver, another Michael (these must be their tourists' names), and a lovely, bouncy, friendly girl in her early 30s called Tracy.

The plan was firstly to go out to the Great Wall at Badaling.

The temperature was now 36°C, thank goodness for the car. At the Great Wall Jo and I went off on our own for a couple of hours. I only went a short way, as it was very steep and the steps were uneven in height, depth and width. How fully-armed soldiers managed to run up and down, and fight when necessary, I will never know. Even more incredible is the wall itself, having been built over 2,300 years by different Emperors, commissioning various sections. Built to prevent invasion and later to protect the Silk Road trade, it was built by thousands of labourers such as soldiers, peasants and captured prisoners. Made from brick, sand and stone, it was an integrated defensive system with fortresses, watchtowers, and communications beacons. This was the most fully restored section of the Great Wall, and most impressive it was too.

I only went so far up and waited whilst Jo continued the climb, by now in temperatures of 40°C. A Chinese man from Hawaii and I found the only section of shade, which we defended from attack, from all quarters, by other hot tourists. The soldiers of old would have been proud of us. Nice guy, we had a laugh. I waited for Jo to come back, but missed her as there was a different path back down.

A quick phone call sorted that out, and we met up again. I called her my hero for her epic climb, and bought her a certificate to mark the occasion. The views were spectacular.

Back in the car we relaxed. Thank goodness for the air-conditioning. On the outward journey we had visited a Jade Factory where we had bought some small pieces to bring home to England. On the return journey we went to a Silk Museum, where we saw a demonstration of how silk was made, the technique first being developed from 3630 BC.

'Silk thread is made by mulberry silk worms whilst making their cocoons. The females can lay several hundred eggs which hatch into larvae. Liquid silk is secreted into the air as the pupae stage is reached, which when hardened is wrapped into the threads. Later the cocoons are dissolved in boiling water so that the threads can be loosened and wrapped on to spinning reels. Threads are spun together and as it is one of the strongest natural fibres, it allows for it to be made into clothes, bedding and material bales.'

The beauty of the resulting silks has to be seen to be believed.

Next stop was the Ming Dynasty tombs, another large complex with a main hall area and museum; then in complete contrast we went to the ultra modern Birds Nest Stadium, travelling through the more built-up, modern sections of Beijing.

At the Stadium complex Jo and I got out for a walk, where we were immediately surrounded by hawkers selling all manner of, shall I say, could be better made, extremely expensive for what it was, tourist goods that we neither liked nor wanted. They would not take no for an answer, to the point where we got angry and went back to the car. I don't think they have got this tourist thing quite right yet. Unfortunately it did not stop there and I got stung for a lot of money. We went for a foot soak at the sports complex, saw a 'doctor' who persuaded me to buy some Chinese medicine, it didn't seem too bad, so I agreed. When it came, it was three months supply, cost a fortune and stupid me went along with it, own fault, embarrassed, but <u>never</u> again. Jo was mortified and had tried her best to stop this happening but sadly to no avail. However, overall the day was very good and we were tired but happy when we got back to our little house. Food, good chat, then bed. A very early start the next day, as we were going to Xi'an.

Day 37 May 29th

We got up at 5 a.m., got a taxi okay, but sadly from there the day went downhill. The train was exciting, a bullet train which travelled at up to 310 km/hr. We had a carriage attendant so it felt rather like being on a plane.

We arrived all excited at Xi'an.

'Capital of the Shaanxi Province in Central China, once known as Chang'an (Eternal Peace). Home to the Han, Qin, Tang and Zhou Dynasties and the world famous Terracotta Army (Bingmayong), buried with China's first Emperor Qin Shi Huang. One of the oldest cities in China, lying at the start of the Silk Road. The original city wall was completed in 190 BC. A city of cultural and religious diversity.'

Unfortunately for us there was no-one we could speak with, no dual language signs, nothing, so we had a terrible time getting out to the site. We were met with lots of shrugs, as if they had never heard of the Terracotta Warriors, which we didn't believe for one moment. We had a confrontation with some Taxi drivers (about 10 of them), who surrounded us, pointing and shouting in our faces. Very intimidating. Finally after the intervention of a transport policeman, one of them said he could take us. It soon became evident that he did not know the way, or he wanted us to believe, when suddenly he pulled over on the motorway hard shoulder and phoned for instructions. A ploy used, we realised later, in many countries, meter still running of course. His driving was erratic and frightening, we began to wonder if we would ever get there.

We were extremely relieved to see the site at last, got out of the taxi with shaky legs, paid him and walked to the site. We were approached by a guide named Marie, with whom we spent 90 minutes, so little time because of our travel restrictions, return train time, but also because of all the nonsense we had endured getting there.

The first sight of the Warriors took our breath away. The Chinese name for them literally means "soldier and horse funerary statues". They were sculptures of the army of Emperor Qin Shi Huang and buried with him in 210-209 BC, to protect him in the afterlife. Three pits, discovered by farmers in 1974, are estimated to have over 8,000 soldiers and their accompanying horses and chariots, originally thought to have been painted to look as life-like as possible. The figures were life sized, varying in their height, features and uniform dependent on rank. In other pits nearby there were the musicians, acrobats and officials, and the excavations were still on-going. There is a line of thought that the sculptures may have been made by western craftsmen. The whole area is thought to cover 38 square miles.

We wandered around a huge covered area, like a massive aircraft hanger. It was absolutely stunning. As we were walking back Marie told us that our taxi driver was waiting. "Oh no" I said. We paid him and besides, after the horrendous outward journey, there was no way we would get back in his taxi. This proceeded to cause a problem as it would potentially impact on the relationship between the taxi drivers and the guides at the site. Bear in mind, that these were the same drivers who supposedly did not know where the site was. I promptly had a panic attack, more real than not this time, and eventually he went. Jo and I sat in the shade to decide what to do. Luckily we found another taxi driver who was far more amenable and knew the way back to the city.

We were very relieved to get back to the station. There we met a very nice local young woman called Vivienne, who was friendly and helpful and she and Jo went off to get us a take-away. We were so happy to get back to our little house in Beijing. The Warriors were magnificent, but the rest of it was a nightmare. It should not have been that traumatic, but still, overall, it was an amazing experience. We had supper, wound down, then went to bed.

Chapter 8

Time for reflection in Beijing

Day 38

Jo left today. We got a very early taxi, arranged by Coffee, so no trouble, to the airport. It was comfortable and air-conditioned so we arrived at the departure lounge very relaxed. I felt sad waving her off as I had really enjoyed her company. I got the shuttle bus back to the main station, then a taxi back home. He got a bit lost around the Hutong area, but I eventually recognised the turning. I think that this time it was genuine; the Hutongs are a maze of very similar looking alleys, and also he appeared to be a nice guy so I did not have my usual feeling of being guarded, of myself or my purse.

I decided to have a house-keeping day, laundry, shopping and general preparations for the arrival of Vicky, even though that wasn't for a couple of days. I needed a rest; I was emotionally wrung out and very hot. Had an afternoon siesta, then I went to the supermarket; well, the little shop in the alley, and after much pointing and shrugging I managed to come home with pretty much what I needed. I am not the best shopper at home, so to do it there was an achievement for me. I made a meal, then watched the TV; I found a film with Jet Li in it with English sub-titles so had a relaxing evening. After that, however, all TV watched was in Chinese, with Chinese sub-titles; different dialects presumably.

Day 39

I had a good sleep, after checking that everything was all locked up, twice. Each room had its own lock, as did the door out to the alley. I got ready slowly as it was far too hot to rush. Thought I would go to Tiananmen

Square. Oh, I spoke with son Simon last night; it was good to speak with him. He told me to watch out for wayward Tanks; speaking of which, Jo and I had seen a goods train at one of the incoming stations, loaded with about 30 Tanks. We wondered where they were going.

I walked down to the square, past the small shops that line the main road, saw all manner of people going about their business, around the outer walls of the Forbidden Kingdom. Such a swirling of people loudly buying and selling their wares against a background of numerous colourful shop windows. I bought a three inch square mirror, beautifully decorated on the back with a scene from Imperial China, perfect handbag size, from one of the shops en-route.

I eventually came to a very wide, busy main road. Was passed by a Jeep with armed soldiers, I guess on their routine sweep of the area; they looked relaxed enough. I used the underpass to get to the other side of the road, and finally reached the Square. There were security gates on all approaches where you and your belongings were scanned. I wandered around the area, mainly a big empty space with occasional sculptures, very large sculptures, depicting scenes of the workers revolution.

Facing the square is an entrance to the Forbidden Kingdom, on which there sat an equally large portrait of Chairman Mao. Flanking the area were two large buildings which I did not visit. The heat by then was just too much for me. Having taken some photos, I sat on a bench between two policemen and two soldiers, all of whom ignored each other, and me, then it was time for home.

I had to stop a few times on the way back, and found whatever I could to sit on. I watched various scenes taking place, including a lot of shouting and gesturing. I guess this was how you made yourself heard in such a large population. A guy with one of the small motorbike type rickshaws, well really a bicycle, stopped and asked if I needed a lift. I said no and plodded on. However, further up the road he came back and asked me again, so after negotiating a small fee he took me up to the alley. When I got in the house and saw myself in the mirror, well, no wonder he was so insistent; I looked as if I was about to collapse at any second. Thank you to him, and I learnt that I am just no good in really hot weather and shouldn't go for such long walks alone.

In fact, the whole trip was a series of revelations, not just of the places I visited, but of any preconceived notions I may have had; also of the local populaces, of my friends all of whom were amazing and really shared in my adventure, and of course, myself, and how to deal with my limitations in situations that I encountered along the way. The thing about getting older as anyone of a certain age group will know, is that although in your head you can achieve anything, you must make allowances for your physical strength not being able to keep up. Oh, I do not mean don't do it; you just need to find a way that accommodates your body as well as your mind. Someone I once knew said "feel the fear, and do it anyway", to which I added my own adage "I'll try anything once, and twice if I like it".

It was now 21.30 and there was a thunder storm and very heavy rain, so I went outside to dance in the courtyard, well no-one could see, back in for a warm shower, pyjamas on and just time to watch some TV before bed. I was watching a war-time type 'soap opera' depicting Chinese local villages fighting the Japanese invasion. There seemed to be a lot of those programmes on, with the locals being the victors. I got quite addicted to one series, even though I could not understand a word.

Chapter 9

Vicky in Beijing, China

"You should have a chat with this new girl. You'll like her, she sounds just your sort of person". A new colleague, ready to become a new friend. I did indeed like her. Another adventurous soul with a love of all things new. Turns out she also did the Husky Charity Challenge Run, two years after I did. Vicky, another 'mad' girl, perfect for this adventure.

Day 40

Vicky was arriving today. I had a leisurely morning getting ready to go to the airport. Having already been with Jo it was no bother getting there. Taxi and shuttle bus. The plane was a little late and finally Vicky came through, poor lass looked absolutely worn out. Big hugs all round. Time to negotiate the return trip to our house. No problem with the shuttle bus, but once again with the gauntlet of taxi drivers, until we were able to battle our way through to the official taxi queue. You had to be a little careful with the ones touting for business. Finally got our address over to the driver, then thankfully home. I made a mental note to myself that if

I ever came to China again, it would with an organised party to smooth the way, or learn the language.

Vicky was pleased to see our home and went off for a well-needed and deserved rest. Once awake we had a good chat about her journey, had some food and watched TV for a while. Oh dear, I had become addicted to my war time 'Sharpe'-like programme, and as Vicky later put it, my 'eye patch' man. Checked over my photos as I did every evening before going to bed. The delete button was getting well used, but even so there were many more being kept. We mused on how to spend our days in Beijing, as we were moving on to the Yellow Mountain region in the following days.

Day 41

We walked down to Tiananmen Square. It was a public holiday, so there were many, many people.

It took us ages to get through the security gates. I wandered around whilst Vicky took photos. I had been already on a far less crowded day. It was so very hot. We walked back through the Mao Gate into the Forbidden City area and up to the South Gate. It was much cooler, because here were trees, walkways, benches and places to have our drinks. This time I was going to be the guide, having learnt from Michael, telling the history as we went along. I showed her the different types of Lion Guardians and how the male was the one with his paw on the ball, and the female with the baby.

Even managed to stave off the various sellers. Many more photographs were taken as we traversed through the City up to the North Gate. We looked into some of the various side chambers where fascinating artefacts were stored. We crossed the main road to the Jinling Gardens where I took Vicky to the Tea Ceremony Pavilion. The girls there recognised me which was lovely, and made us both very welcome. We thoroughly enjoyed the time in there.

Everywhere was so much busier and a number of people took our photos as we wandered around. It struck me that they may have thought that Vicky was a Geisha due to her doll-like features. Whatever the reason many pictures were taken. When we came out, we got a motorised Rickshaw home and were each given a hug by the driver. We came in, had our tea meal, then tried to get some travel information printed off from my Tablet, but to no avail. A man and his daughter from the local computer place down the Alley were very nice and helpful and restored my faith in people after the various horrific encounters with the taxi drivers. We watched TV for a while, well I had to get my war-time soap opera fix. And then to bed, needed an earlyish night, as we had a full day ahead.

Day 42

We became used to the place, and especially loved the area where we were living, even getting smiles from the local people, (but we won't talk about the taxi drivers). Arranged another day out with Tracy, as Jo and I had really enjoyed our time with her and her driver. Firstly we made all the introductions; she was fascinated by Vicky and kept saying how pretty she was, and she was right. We went out to the Great Wall, but this time to Mu Tian Yu where there was a cable car, so I was able to go much higher. As expected, the views were absolutely stunning; I could not fault the Country for the magnificent vistas everywhere.

We walked for quite some time, up and down steps. Again I thought about the workers building the wall; what a feat of engineering, and also of the soldiers who lived, defended and fought where necessary on the wall. It was beyond my comprehension.

We went back down to meet up with Tracy. We had fun on the cable car; on the way up, we struck poses and had a good laugh. Vicky and I were very similar in that way, with a love of the bizarre. The way down, of course was very different. We had spotted a toboggan run from the cable car, so I just knew that was going to be our exit strategy, down the rather steep hillside.

It was time to grab my courage by its ears and throw caution to the speed gathering wind. At the terminal there was a board listing a number of things (health-wise), prohibiting people from using that form of transport. After the first five answers were yes, I stopped reading it. I reckoned I was well covered, having taken all of my pills that morning.

When it got to my turn to be loaded into what looked like a small silver tray, the operator asked me my age.

"How old, lady?"

"67" I said.

"How old, lady?"

"67".

And again he asked, but before I could get annoyed, he looked around, rolled his eyes, then said "how old lady, 60, 59?"

Oh, I thought, of course, 67 was too old. ""59" I said confidently.

"Good" he said. "Get in"

Well what an experience. The tray had a lever which applied the brakes when needed, but after the first few bends, I just let it go at its own speed. It reminded me of when I had my motorbike years ago, leaning into the bends. Such great fun. I heard Vicky coming down behind me, laughing all the way.

On the way back into Beijing we visited a Cloisonne factory. It was interesting watching the items being made, such beautiful decorative works where enamel, gemstones or glass, on a metal backplate, were separated by strips of flattened wire. Very delicate work being done by the skilled workforce. Of course the usual hard sell happened, but by now I was getting better at resisting.

Next stop was the Summer Palace, but on the way the car broke down so we had to transfer to a taxi to take us to our next stop at Dr. Tea. Another Tea Ceremony, but I have to say, although beautifully done, it to my mind was not as good as the one at Jinling Gardens. Then on to the Summer Palace area. A stunning location; no wonder the Emperor and his family would go there for a break from the Forbidden City. We went across the Lake in a Dragon Boat, a nice gentle crossing with spectacular views, absolutely beautiful.

Speaking of which, in the car Tracy sang the James Blunt song 'Beautiful' with us all joining in at the chorus. Spontaneous and lovely.

We walked back through the decorated arches around the side of the Lake.

A local tourist asked to take photographs of us, so feeling like celebrities, we obliged. Then we got a Rickshaw back to the car park, where our newly repaired car was waiting for us. A quick trip to a Pearl Factory and home. A very full day, most enjoyable, but we were glad to be home. The heat really sapped our energy, so there had to be lots of stops, certainly in my case.

We watched some TV whilst we were winding down. I fancied some supper which Vicky volunteered to get. She returned with a bowl of cherries and ice cream, and, a pair of chopsticks; very funny. So what did I do? Well, ate the lot, of course. We packed our things ready to move on to the Yellow Mountains, and then to bed.

Chapter 10

Journey to the Yellow Mountains

Day 43

Coffee was coming for us around 11 a.m., so after breakfast we packed our last few things and cleaned the house. We were sorry to be leaving it; we had enjoyed the time here very much, both Jo and Vicky. She was kindly going to take our main luggage to her town flat to store for us until we got back, after which we were getting the TransManchurian train to Moscow on Day 47, June 7th. We were now going to the Yellow Mountains scenic area.

We were really excited about going to this area, and more than a little apprehensive about the journey as the planning for this had been done using an atlas and train timetables. A real leap of faith, especially on Vicky's behalf, as she had trusted in my organising skills. We had a little time left to take a look over Beijing spread out in all its glory and to remember that the city was made up of very new sections as well as its old heritage spaces.

We were going via Shanghai for a few days, so we only took our backpacks. Firstly though, we needed to pick up our tickets for the Moscow train. Walking along outside the alley, we wondered whether to take the chance of getting a taxi; could we stand being ripped off again? Vicky suddenly hailed a rickshaw driver, one of the type with a motorised bicycle front and two seats at the back. We asked if he would take us and to our surprise, he said that he would. A big jovial guy with a lovely smile. We negotiated the price, as it was quite a long way from where we were, then off we went.

Wow, what a journey; it was exhilarating and scary at the same time. We went down main roads, sometimes on the correct side of the road, down the sidewalks horn blaring when the roads were busy, across the junctions whether the lights were green or not, and through parts of the city we had never seen before and finally to our destination, stopping right outside where we needed to be. Amazing, and even more amazingly, he charged us the quoted price. We were very impressed and of course gave him a huge tip, which he had well earned. Really enjoyed the whole experience; it was the best public-type transport trip during my whole stay in China. Now that was fun.

We picked up our tickets with no trouble. The procedure was painless, so at least we knew we could get to our next main destination. This also came with the realisation that once on the Moscow train, we would be starting the return journey to England.

From there we got the subway to the Beijing West Station for the overnight train to Shanghai. We had a few hours to spare, so we spent the time wandering around the area, looking at the shops, arcades and generally people-watching, as they went about their daily lives, whether it be on foot, in cars or on heavily laden bicycles. I do not know how they balance, with so many goods or family perched precariously on them.

After eating, we went back to the station and boarded the train at 20.55, found our cabin which we were to share with a woman and her eight year old son, and a man who spoke no English; and why should he in his own country, but he smiled a lot.

After some chat with the lady, we settled down for the night in our comfortable bunks, and thought about what the next part of the adventure might bring for us.

Chapter 11

Huang Shan

Day 44

We woke up quite refreshed, our nice travelling companions shared their breakfast with us. We came off the train and needed to find the station where we could board the train for Hangzhou. We met a rather strange, but helpful guy in the station who insisted on taking us to our next connection point, Hangquo station. He spoke English and took us the whole journey, which I must say was a little worrying at first, but we decided that in the end he was okay. It was a long way and involved getting two different Metro lines. We paid him a little money, although he did not ask us for any, but to be honest he looked as if a good meal would benefit him.

The journey to Hangzhou was uneventful, once we got the right tickets. Our first attempt nearly sent us off to the wrong place, but a station worker helped us. The journey took about four hours.

'Hangzhou was a very busy place, a city 155 miles away from Shanghai and capital of the Zhejiang Province and sits at the head of the Hangzhou bay separating Shanghai and Ningbo. Tea has been an important part of the city's economy, especially a variety of green tea known as Longjing. An area of natural beauty.'

Our next challenge was to find the Bus Station, for the rest of the journey to Huang Shan. After a few failed attempts to get directions, we met a guy sitting on a scooter who told us we had to go on a local bus (no. 41) out to the main Bus Terminal. He followed us to make sure we got to the right stop. Very helpful. The local bus came, and we were off. It got more and more crowded and hot as the journey progressed and finally after an hour we got to our destination. Must say we caused quite a stir on the bus. We queued for our outgoing tickets and were told that the bus was just about to leave in three minutes, and was the last one of the day. *Oh no*, I thought, *I can't run for that*, especially as it was from another section of the station, but Vicky had faith and was sure we would make it. We arrived at 15.02 (it was due to leave at 15.00) but it had been delayed. Thank you providence.

We settled into our seats and off we went, the beginning of a six hour journey, through some spectacular scenery, past small towns, rivers, villages nestling in the hills and small farms dotted everywhere.

As I said previously, every bit of land that could be cultivated was, for just that purpose. We went through a number of tunnels, each getting progressively longer. Each one was named but before I could alert Vicky, we went through one called the Shitaloonga tunnel, *very aptly named*, I thought. We finally arrived at Huang Shan, well, not quite there, at a small town named Tangkou.

It was 11 p.m., so we were very fortunate to meet a man, Mr. Hu, who took us in his car to our hotel. Where were these sort of people in Beijing? Really nice hotel where once we had settled in, made us a meal. Sadly we weren't as hungry as we thought, so didn't eat much. Then to bed, and a really good sleep.

Day 45

We woke refreshed, had a good breakfast, such an important meal for me, I can't start my day without it. Next we needed to find where the local bus left from, up to the Huang Shan Mountains. A well known area of natural beauty, steeped in history, and often used as the subject of traditional Chinese paintings. There was a cable car system in operation to link the town with the summits. It pleased me as hill climbing was not my thing, not enough breath or muscle tone.

The hotel minibus took us up to the little bus station. We got our tickets and sat back and enjoyed the journey. It took about 30 minutes through beautiful scenery, then what a sight greeted us; the Yellow Mountains stretching out. We went up to a vantage point on a cable car. Spectacular; what an amazing place. Named as a UNESCO World Heritage Site in 1990, it was located in the Anhui Province.

The area was made up of various peaks with beautiful names such as Dawn Pavilion, Lion Peak, Rosy Clouds Peak, Peach Blossom Peak, Lotus Blossom Peak, Jade Screen Peak amongst many others. Pine trees, unique to the area, grew from the very steep slopes, and there were over a hundred rock formations with outlines that resembled people and animals. The view was said to change with each season, each one with its own particular beauty. These were the views that can often be seen on the walls of Chinese restaurants and chip shops in the UK. Again, it was an experience coming to life before me, not just in paintings. Breathtakingly beautiful.

A walkway had been built around a winding track, in keeping with the area, log and cobble steps and wooden balustrades.

I walked as far as I could, then turned back. Sadly, Vicky hurt her ankle so her progress was slow and painful from then on. She could have done with the sedan chair we saw being carried by two, very hot men; they must have really earned their money that day. We did however manage to take lots of photographs.

We wandered slowly back through the forest to the bus area and got what we thought was the same bus back to the bus station, except it wasn't. This one went to another station in Huang Shan town, outside of the scenic area. We spoke with a cafe owner there, who after the arrangement of a very small fee, took us back to our part of the town. Bit tricky those buses. Still, everything was done in a very good-natured way.

We collected our luggage and went to where the Shanghai bus was leaving from, a sort of cafe/roadhouse where there was a direct bus, so we did not have to change at Hangzhou. Time was not too critical, as we had booked into a hotel in Shanghai for the night, just as well as we waited a few hours for the bus, but no matter, as there was enough to keep us occupied, eating, resting and taking photographs, and generally re-living our experiences.

The bus finally arrived, not luxurious in any way, but hey, the driver was a real character. We found our seats and settled back for the seven to eight hour journey. We saw some amazing scenery on the journey; it was good to see rural China as well as the cities, made us feel much more connected to the country and its people.

In our imagination, there were some shady deals going on, boxes being off-loaded at roundabouts where people emerged out of the undergrowth. Could, of course, been a form of postal delivery service, but we liked our version better. The bus got into the terminal after 11 p.m. We saw a policeman who directed us to the taxi rank; however, a lady who was standing nearby said she would take us to the hotel. We assumed she was a taxi driver. Poor Vicky was limping badly as her foot had really swollen up. We all went outside the station, where we waited and waited. We could see the other taxis, but she had hold of Vicky and it was not as if we could run anywhere. The taxi finally arrived with two men in already; we got in and so did the lady. We started to get panicky, but thought it must be alright because the policeman was present when she said about the taxi. They took us to the hotel, but it was a very worrying journey. We vowed we would never do that again.

The hotel thankfully was lovely, a 5* palace, very much what we needed at that juncture. First things first, I unpacked while Vicky had a bath, then vice versa. A strange day all around, we were very glad of our comfortable beds.

Day 46

The hotel sadly was a long way from the centre of Shanghai.

I had chosen it because it was in the same district as the Bus Station, which I had believed to be in the city centre. The consequence was that we did not have time for sightseeing in the city before it was time for our return rail journey to Beijing, and from there on to Moscow. We were sorry, we had looked forward to that.

Another Bullet train ride; we had good seats and sat next to a young local guy called Nick, who was studying abroad but was home on holiday. His English was excellent, so we had an interesting, chatty journey back.

We arrived about 4 p.m. at Beijing main station, then got the Metro near to our little house location. We had a meal in the hotel at the end of the alley, it was very pleasant; soup from inside a big crusty roll, very novel. There was also a viewing platform there, which looked out over the Forbidden Kingdom.

We phoned Coffee and husband John for instructions of where to pick up the rest of our luggage. Our train to Moscow was due at 23.00.

We hailed a Rickshaw but he dropped us off at the wrong place, and he even tried to rip us off. What was wrong with these people? That was where our worst nightmare began. We were completely lost and it took several hours and numerous phone calls for us all to meet up. We got a taxi back to their flat for the luggage, then on to the mainline station. The driver stopped the wrong side of an extremely busy road, so we had to get all of the luggage over a high flyover bridge. Poor Vicky did all the heavy lifting, as I had run out of oomph (and patience) by then.

Finally, we, all bags and baggage were in the station and on to the train. Thank Goodness, or words to that effect. We had both well had enough. We settled into our cabin, and fell into a restless sleep. Exhausted. We were not even aware of the train leaving the station. We had by then had enough of China, but to be fair the scenery was spectacular; some of the people were friendly and welcoming, but a lot of the time I felt uncomfortable. On this occasion I was glad to leave. I think I would like to go again, but with an organised party, but then I might not get the same sense of adventure and discovery as I had this time.

However, we did get to see some amazing things and had some very good experiences. I should mention some of the people who made the trip worthwhile; Tracy our guide and her driver, Michael the Forbidden City guide, the helpful lady in Huang Shan, Mr. Hu in Tangkou, Vivienne at Xi'an railway station, our eccentric guide through the Metro stations, the motorbike Rickshaw man and mostly Coffee and John, our house owners for their help with everything.

Chapter 12

Train back to Moscow

Day 47 June 8th

I woke up, feeling much better rested. The TransManchurian route was slightly longer than the outgoing one was with Jo. I cannot believe that this was now the return half of the trip, but I have to say I have had the most amazing time so far, and I didn't think that this section was going to be any different.

Vicky and I set about making our cabin home, as it would be for the next week. We sorted out the food and packed away what was not needed under the seats. We spent the rest of the time getting dressed and just watched the world go by, comfortable on our beds, as we watched the early morning workers on their work, all the time being gently rocked by the train.

We spent the day relaxing, playing card games, doing crosswords, just as Jo and I had done, and of course taking photographs. No trees as yet to leap into the photos, but of course this was still China so we were looking at towns and housing estates, which here were multi-storey tower blocks.

It was 15.00 and we had reached Harbin. A place well known throughout the world for its Ice and Snow Festival in January to mid-March, sadly not something we were able to see at this time of year. The city links Beijing with the city of Chita, in a region originally inhabited by Mongolic and Turkic tribes, in Eastern Siberia, where the railway line linked up with the TransSiberian line, which was where we are now headed.

Once out of the cities we were again struck by the amount of agriculture that was going on in every available tiny space. Also I had never seen so many high rise buildings, mostly for the moment, empty. We snacked all day, and finally settled down when it went dark. It was nice to ease back into the travelling; this train was a lot smoother running than the previous one had been. And so to sleep.

Day 48

We got woken up, quite unceremoniously by the Chinese Border Guards. Must be all of 4 a.m. Out of bed and into the corridor. They searched everything. They were a bit perplexed by one of our food items; it unfortunately had a picture with an armed soldier on it. In the end I opened it for them; it was instant porridge. Smiles all around, thank goodness; we didn't want to be arrested over our breakfast choice.

It felt as if we had just gone back to sleep when the door was flung open again, this time by the Russian Border Guards. They took ages checking all of our documents, Visas, Passports etc. Then a guard with the cutest dog came strolling down the corridor. *Awh* I thought, *how sweet, he's come to work with his pet.* Shows how naïve I was; it was a sniffer dog of course. They also went through our cabin. They weren't worried by our porridge, must have seen it before. Thankfully all was ok. Even though we knew we had nothing we shouldn't have, it was still worrying. The whole thing made us kind of nervous even though we had nothing to be nervous about (we had obviously read too many 'spy' books). Next the Customs People arrived and went through everything again. Then suddenly it was all quiet.

We didn't have much time to relax because as with the outward journey, the wheels on the carriages needed to be changed back to the Russian gauge. We had got washed and changed by then. As it was daylight, we had to get off the train and wait on the platform. It was a long few hours.

Carriage by carriage was taken off to the train shed and returned being pulled along by a brightly painted shunting engine.

Finally we were off; time for Brunch, then back to surveying the scenery. We had gone on to Moscow time and I was a little confused as to how long we had been up. We spent the rest of the day gazing out of the window, taking photos and watching the eastern world slip into the distance as we continued our journey westwards. I managed a cat nap in there somewhere too.

Day 49

The train had been stopped in the forest for quite some time.

Vicky was still asleep and I had been taking some early morning pictures, before the noisy family from down the corridor were up and about, not that they were any trouble, they were not. I did not know where we were until we got to a station, but before that it was good to just sit in the quiet looking at the trees. People certainly start their days very early in this part of the world. We watched rail workers maintaining the lines, and also women coming down from the forest villages to catch the local trains to market.

The man in the next cabin seemed to go down to the toilet at the end of the carriage as often as me, but I think in his case it was for a sneaky cigarette. The train had taken off again; we were both up, washed, dressed and had even washed our 'smalls', which were drying off around the cabin. We hoped there would be no more 'official' visits.

We were skirting Lake Baikal and even though it was the second time for me, I was still overawed by the stunning views.

I think Vicky must have set her camera on rapid shot as all I could hear was the shutter, either that or she was blessed with very fast eye to finger coordination. We thought we would go up to the Restaurant car for our evening meal, so of course, we 'dressed up' to make a proper occasion of it.

We passed through Irkutsk, one of the largest Siberian cities, where the first Siberian road was built in 1760. It became a major centre of social and intellectual life for Decembrist exiles. By 1900 the city had earned the nickname "Paris of Siberia". During the Russian Civil War it was the scene of many "Red" and "White" army clashes.

Later, we had a very nice meal, Salmon, which was very tasty. I had a bit of a lost in translation moment when asking for a Coca Cola. The waiter said "American". I said "Yes" then I got an extremely strong American coffee, oops. Vicky had it in the end, as this particular traveller is a dedicated tea drinker. Apart from that short sojourn we had spent the day taking photos, or at least, attempting to take them.

A little story: Vicky, fed up with getting pylons, goods trains and trees in her photos, asked me to stand guard and tell her when we reached a clear clearing, she being finger on trigger so to speak.

"Right" I said "Clearing coming up, 3,2,1..."

Click, Click, Click. *oh good*, I thought, *job done*.

When she reviewed the pictures there was a "Oh no, I thought you said it was clear".

"It was" I said.

"Well" she said indignantly, "what are these then?"

There, in the absolute centre of her photo, were two trees, standing in a perfect 'V' formation, as if mocking the pair of us. Had they have been able to speak, we could imagine what the derisive comment would have been. I was sure that the clearing, right through to the lakeside had been clear, so the trees must have been lying in wait, ready to pop up, as we passed by. Only explanation. We did laugh.

Having made other abortive attempts throughout the day, she realised that you just have to live with whatever is lurking unseen in the vista.

As we again reached the forests she turned and said "Oh, I give in. I am going to photograph the trees". A few clicks later, there was a huge explosion of "I don't believe it!" There, in the middle of her beautiful forest picture. a house had jumped into the frame, and that, of course, was the end of the photo session for that day.

Day 50 June 11th

I woke up early again, as I had slept fitfully. Still, no worries; it wasn't as if I had to be somewhere at any certain time. Quite liked looking out of the window and taking the odd photo before the day had really started.

Later we had almost a breakfast feast; porridge and banana, crisp type bread and tea, it was good. As I previously said, having hot water on tap 24/7 meant that a brew could be made at any time. I put the blind back down and went back to sleep for a while. What luxury, no clocks, alarms, or work schedules to worry about, just able to please ourselves all day. And that was just what we did. We spent the day talking, playing Hangman, cards, doing crosswords, all of our usual things.

Stood at the window to see Krasnoyarsk, the third largest city in Siberia and one of the places where political exiles were sent, including the eight Decembrists deported from St. Petersburg after the failure of the revolt. During Stalinist times it was a major centre of the Gulag system, and later in the 1990s it became the location of a large Aluminium Plant.

We saw a beautiful rainbow after a rain storm, and then a beautiful sunset, although I still haven't seen one anywhere that rivals the sunsets over West Kirby and New Brighton on the Wirral and I have been around a bit, figuratively speaking.

Day 51

I had a better sleep. This was going to be our last full day on the train. We saw the obelisk that marked the end, or for some the beginning of Siberia, previous 'place of tears'.

The train was about to arrive at Ykaterinburg. On the return journey, places Jo and I had seen at night, Vicky and I were to see in daylight. The day went by very quickly; we were still trying to take photographs whilst dodging the various obstacles, even a smoke screen from who knew what or where. It was our last sleep on the train, we had become kind of used to it, and I knew I would miss the rocking of the carriage, the clanking of the wheels on the tracks and the general noises of train life. Guess what we had for our tea, yep, noodles. I don't think I will ever want them again once home. I felt very tired, so it was early to bed.

Chapter 13

Arrival back in Moscow with Vicky

Day 52

It was the last day on the train and I actually managed to sleep well. I had a wash, then with breakfast all done, it was time to repack everything ready to disembark at Moscow. How quickly the days have gone. I could not believe it. Had the same feeling that Jo and I had arriving in Beijing, sorry to leave the cosy little 'home' that we had just shared for the last seven days.

So hello Moscow (second time for me) and promptly got ripped off by yet another taxi driver. Even gave him the address of the hotel in Russian, made me want to scream! The same little ploy was used, not knowing the way, asking for instructions, wandering off for ten minutes with the meter running. The worst thing was that they thought they were fooling you. This happened in other countries too, grrr.

The hotel was a bit spartan, a room in the annex of an old church, but never mind. Vicky was convinced it was part of a brothel, I was not so sure. (Not that either of us had ever been in one, you understand, just seen too many films). We watched TV for a bit, unpacked what we needed, and after food brought from our stash on the train, we lay on our beds, talked, sorted photos and finally fell asleep.

Day 53 June 14th

We awoke. Breakfast was brought to the room on a tray, and was surprisingly good; cereal, juice, toast, and not a noodle or instant porridge in sight. We dressed ready to meet the challenges of the day.

We went to Red Square after we had studied the Metro routes. Once there, I was able to show Vicky around. I felt like a local as everything was very familiar. She was very impressed with the square and its buildings. We went into the Historical museum and spent a few hours there learning about Moscow and Russian culture/life generally. We spent the rest of the day in and around Red Square, went to the market type stalls where we bought souvenirs to take home, which included a fur army type hat for Vicky, very fetching, and then to a circle in the pavement outside the main gate where you stood and threw coins over your shoulder.

Legend said that if you did so, you would return to Moscow. The place was surrounded by elderly ladies, who moved like lightning to retrieve the coins.

We found a cafe and then decided to walk back to the hotel. Funny, it never seemed very far when you had used some form of transport, but the walking distance was a different matter. The hotel was at the opposite end of Moscow to where the flat had been, and was overall in a far less salubrious area, but still interesting for all of that. We took some food back to the room, reminisced about the day, then bed. We were still a little 'train lagged'.

Day 54

A new day so we decided to go on the HoHo buses and a boat trip through central Moscow, on the Moskva river. Luckily we took our waterproof plastic ponchos. Well, did it rain, oh yes. We found the bus stop and went down to the river area for the boat. We both took some photos of the local area; it was good to see other parts of the city, not just the touristy bits. So, on to the boat; we started off in pretty clear weather, but 20 minutes down river a huge black cloud loomed overhead. Having previously taken off our ponchos, we decided to reinstate them.

The rain started and the other passengers fled into the covered section of the boat. We stayed put. What was a little rain to us? We were made of sterner stuff; we were from the U.K. Well, the rain got heavier and heavier and still we stayed outside, taking our photos, laughing, much to the amusement of the other passengers. However the Russian weather was not to be outdone, and decided to add hail into its arsenal, gently at first and then more and more and more; boy did it hail with chunks of ice in increasing sizes. So okay, it got to the point where even us hardened English had to shelter. We got into the cabin area to a round of applause and dissolved into a bout of laughter from which we could not stop. A Chinese tourist was most amused and took photos of us, telling us we were his heroes.

We went back to the hotel, got changed, well yes, we were soaked, but still laughing. We went out again later to find the Soviet Bunker (No. 42) that Vicky had found on-line. Again it looked really close, but...

The bunker was very interesting. There was no English-speaking guide available so we tagged along with a Russian party. To be fair, most of it was self-explanatory, with an exceptionally explicit film of what happened in a nuclear attack. It was harrowing. Towards the end of the tour we went down a long tunnel and suddenly the sirens went off, the doors clanged shut and the whole place was plunged into darkness and silence. Talk about a shock. After what seemed an age, a red light came on.

The look of horror on everyone's faces was genuine. We found the whole experience really interesting, but scary. Again examples of Man's war-faring nature, and mistrust of fellow beings, and situations that could quickly and easily get out of control. We had quite an in-depth discussion when we got back to the hotel, and in my case anyway, a fitful dream/nightmare-laden sleep.

Day 55

We had to move hotels. The original plan was to go by train to Romania, but because of the Ukraine situation, we were having to fly there. The revolution had taken place there some months previously, therefore given the instability of the country and popular discontent still rising, we were unable to obtain train tickets.

So as to keep the rest of our timetable as planned, we decided to spend the extra days in Moscow, arriving in Bucharest on schedule. We packed and took our cases to the left luggage at Belorusskaya station. So it was back onto the HoHos (just loved them), and a trip down to the Canal area. I took Vicky to see the park statues (see Day 28 for information), then went onto the bridge and across the canal. Vicky had bought a 'love lock' that she wanted to place there, so with due ceremony that little task was carried out.

We spent the rest of the day sightseeing, then went back to get our luggage ready to move on to the airport hotel. It was a really nice place, good room and then, as we were both tired out, a shower and an early night.

Day 56

We went out for the early transport bus into Moscow. Due to our forced change of plans we were staying here for three nights before flying to Romania. Once back in the city we decided to visit the Novodevichy Cemetery on the outskirts of Moscow.

'This is the most famous cemetery in Moscow, lying next to the walls of the 16th century convent, designed in 1898 by Ivan Mashov. Since the fall of the Soviet Union only the most symbolically significant burials have taken place there. Prior to that, and to date there are about 27,000 buried there including Poets, Musicians, Authors, Actors, Playwrights, Scientists, Military notables and Politicians such as Bresnev and Krushchev.'

It was quite a long journey to get there, but as stated, Russian transport was very good. Once we finally arrived, we got some sandwiches from a little shop near the station exit, which we then shared with the local sparrows in a small park.

The Cemetery itself was amazing, so much to see with all the decorated grave stones and even though we couldn't read what was on them, it didn't matter. There were many interesting statues, big and small throughout the grounds, large monuments and a number of chapels.

Vicky and I both managed to scare a party of Japanese tourists, me by sitting very still on the cornerstone of one of the graves, and then moving, must have looked paler than I thought. Vicky, well she did it by bursting through the undergrowth, having just found the perfect photo opportunity. There was an intake of collective breath that even I heard on the other side of the area. I don't suppose it helped that Vicky, with her black hair, white face and goth type clothes, looked just the part to be bursting out from between the gravestones. Once together, we just laughed and laughed. A huge place, we could have stayed there all day, but decided to do more sightseeing in Central Moscow instead, or to be more technically correct, under Central Moscow.

The Metro stations were fascinating and most of them had plaques, statues and/or paintings, so we thought we would travel around the system looking and photographing what we saw; no goods trains or trees to leap out here. It was all very impressive. Some time earlier I had seen an Arts Programme on TV with Andrew Dixon talking about the art of the underground stations and I remember thinking that I would like to see that, and now here I was.

Other fascinating features were the tiny shops situated in the road underpasses. I had never seen so many goods packed into such small areas.

As with China every available space was utilised for commercial or personal use.

We had our meal in the Hard Rock Cafe and met a lovely waitress, Tasha. We enjoyed the food and even joined in with the singing; there was a teenage party going on on the floor below, which we could see from the balcony. We had a great time. This turned out to be one of a number of HRCs that I visited with various friends. We came back to the hotel on the airport express, had a nightcap cocktail and then to bed.

Day 57

Our last day for sightseeing, we were off to Bucharest the next day. We went to the Alexander Gardens, walked around taking in the beautiful colours and the fragrant smells of the flowers, then we played amongst the fairytale statues distributed around the gardens.

Later we queued to get into the Kremlin, only to be told that they had reached their quota for the day. Shame, we shouldn't have left it until our last day.

We went out to the Old Arbat, a street rather like that of Bold Street in Liverpool, with cafes, street art, musicians and colourful young people, (and older ones too).

A vibrant place where we felt quite at home and enjoyed our traverse up the whole length of the street. We saw Tsoi's wall, a graffiti covered wall dedicated to Viktor Tsoi, who sadly died at 28, he and his band Kino were pioneers of Russian rock music.

We got the overland train back to the airport area, took photos of the track side graffiti, and I actually saw a graffiti artist at work for the first time ever, but was too slow with my camera finger. Missed him and the wall, but I got a great picture of a grassy bank. Took my last photograph of Moscow fading into the distance.

Back at the hotel we used the leisure facilities, the pool, sauna, steam room and Jacuzzi, very relaxing, no all-in wrestlers to contend with this time. We had a meal, a drink and then a last minute check that everything was packed properly and bed.

Chapter 14

My travelling companion was still Vicky. We were having so much fun, and were now off to Romania.

Day 58 June 19th

I had a restless night, I was worried about getting up early, I suppose. As it happened, all went well. We went for our Aeroflot flight to Romania. We both would have preferred to go by train, but there was just no travelling over Ukraine due to the situation there. We were sorry, for the land, its people and us. In a strange way I was also sad to be leaving Russia; I had enjoyed the experience much more than I had imagined I would. So it was goodbye Moscow and who knows, a return trip may be in my destiny; I did throw the coin after all.

We had a good flight, but arrived in Bucharest during a downpour. We got a taxi from the airport to the hotel, great system where you just went to the booth, selected the desired price tariff, pressed the button and the machine printed you a ticket telling you which was your designated taxi and how long it would be before it arrived. And well, would you believe, we actually met a good guy, helpful, informative, spoke English and gave us the full tourist blurb on the way to the hotel, and only charged us the agreed fee - wow. Naturally we gave him a large tip, for such good service.

I had booked us into a lovely little bijou type hotel, friendly staff and a good room which overlooked the front of the hotel with a balcony at each window. We unpacked, then explored the surrounding area; thankfully it had stopped raining, before we came in for an evening meal, which was very tasty and plenty of it. We went up to the room and spent some time watching the city light up, and then all go quiet. That was except us who carried on talking, and writing our diaries. It was great to just chill. More sightseeing the next day. We just knew we were going to like it here.

Day 59

I woke up after a good sleep. We had a lovely big breakfast that set us up for the day. The staff, as I said were all friendly and helpful. Vicky had woken up relaxed too. So then it was off for some sightseeing. We decided to go around the local area first, saw a little park-type space where there were tables set out for chess players. Wandered around more and found a small church which was open. There was a lay person there, named Constantine, who was rightly proud of his church and who told us of the history of the place, and allowed us to take some photographs.

Next we decided to walk down into the centre, which was not too far from our hotel. We came across a newly opened cafe called the Art Cafe. What an amazing place, done out like the drawing room of a French château. Vicky had a rose lemonade and I had a pink hot chocolate.

What an experience; it was truly wonderful, delicious and an incredible memory in the making. We carried on down to the centre and found a HoHo for a trip around the city.

'Bucharest is the capital and economic centre of Romania, located in the south of the country. Became the capital in 1862, but first mentioned in manuscripts in 1459. Between the two world wars, it was nicknamed 'little Paris' due to its elegant architecture. Sadly during Ceausescu's leadership (1965 – 1989), a large area of the city was torn down and replaced with developments designated 'Socialist realism' such as the Central Civic and Palace of the Parliament'. An entire historic area was destroyed to make way for the new buildings. The largest Parliament building houses, the Chambre of Deputies and the Senate, as well as the National Museum of Contemporary Art.

'Since 2000 the city has undergone modernisation and urban renewal. There are two internationally renowned Ethnographic Museums including the outdoor Dimitrie Gusti National Village. Many communist era buildings have been restored and reused for other purposes, some having been left in their original state for tourism purposes.'

There was plenty to see. I must admit I had been put off by a certain member of the 'Pythons' who did a programme there; our experience couldn't have been more different. The city had many different types of buildings, some of formal design and some that showed the city's sense of humour with quirky little statues that adorned the facades. Also there were large statues, mostly dedicated to WWII or to the events of 1989. We ended up at an Irish bar for a drink, in my case, tea, and a cake. I was not adverse to drinking, I had just had an extremely bad experience with alcohol poisoning, (under the counter spirits) some years previously, which had put me off for life. We walked slowly back up the hill to the hotel and took in the local sights of the general area, both people and buildings.

Both Vicky and I liked to see the contrasts in life styles in the cities we had visited. We got back just before a thunderstorm hit. We watched the lightning from our beds, each of which faced a balcony.

We spent time talking about what we had done and seen in the past few weeks, which by then included China, Trans Manchurian/TransSiberian Expresses, Moscow and Romania. What a trip; I was having the most amazing time with the friends I had already seen and those still to come. Once again I thought, how I was lucky to know such amazing people.

Day 60

Another day on the HoHos, but this time we stopped off at the open air Folk Museum.

This was an area like Skansen, that Gill and I had visited in Stockholm, but somewhat warmer. We saw many different houses from different eras; we were interested to see how the interiors differed from area to area. We spent most of the day there, enjoying the sunshine, eating and watching the folk dancing displays. We discovered there was a Hard Rock cafe on the site, so of course we just had to go, having enjoyed the one in Moscow so much. We were really tired, but happy when we returned to the hotel, all that fresh air, I guess.

Day 61 June 22nd

It was another moving day, going north to Brasov. This was a city located in the central region of the country, surrounded by the southern Carpathian mountains, part of Transylvania, yes, it really existed, and beautiful scenery it was too. It was first mentioned in documents from 1252, and was the seat of local government for that area. Strongly tied in with the stories of Vlad Tepes, (known as Vlad the Impaler), although the stories of the vampire Dracula supposedly based on Vlad, were 'figments of the imagination' of Irishman Bram Stoker. However the real Vlad had ruled over the area and had visited the various castles situated around his kingdom, including Bran Castle, a fortress on the border of Transylvania and Wallachia. This was erroneously thought to be the home of the man himself, the castle being of a Gothic style, and so it fitted very well into the legend.

We had a good train journey from Bucharest, and of course it always helped when the seats were reserved. We arrived at the station, looked for a taxi to the hotel and sadly one of the younger drivers tried to rip us off. However he was no match for Vicky, we being seasoned travellers by now, so argued the price. Another older guy stepped in and offered us a much more reasonable price. A big bear of a man, but we both liked him and felt safe with him.

On the way he heard us talking about going to Bran Castle the next day. He told us, that like all museums, it was closed on a Monday. We were disappointed as we had very limited time there, so he made us an offer, which we did not refuse, that he could take us there straight away. We were worried about the luggage, as it was in the car boot. "No problem" he said and the deal was done.

The castle was about 30kms from Brasov. We negotiated a reasonable price; he said he would go off for a meal then wait for us as we went around the castle. When we arrived at the car park, he got us to take a photograph of the car and him, so that we knew who/what to look for. This gave us very much more faith in him and our safety. A nice guy, John, we liked him very much.

Our first view of the castle did not disappoint.

The castle was amazing, it was advertised as being Vlad Dracul's castle, but as stated, it was not his main abode. Having said that, it did not detract from our experience there. It very much looked the part, and there were artefacts that had belonged to the man himself, including a letter in his own hand. We loved it.

We found our driver and then it was back to town. We thanked him, paid and asked for his card so we could use him for our return to the station when we were leaving.

Our hotel was called the Vlad Tepes, which had pictures of said man, everywhere. As Brasov sat within the Carpathians you could not come to the area and not be involved in the myths, legends, and some truths about Vlad (Dracul).

Again, a nice hotel, we had some food, unpacked and went out again for a walk around the main square.

We went to the Black Church, so called because of the fire of 1689 which left the church charred.

We went inside, weren't supposed to take photos, but when did that ever stop anyone taking the odd, sneaky, non-flash one? Back at the hotel, more food, then settled in for the night. It had been quite an eventful day, so we were tired.

Day 62

This was a Monday, and as said the museums were all closed, so we went for a walk around the town.

We came across a memorial park where all the people had been killed in the uprisings of 1989, (the disintegration of the Russian Federation and the revolutions which took place in the various satellite states as they fought for sovereignty). We saw many memorials attesting to that event throughout all of the Communist countries that we had previously visited.

We managed to get partly up Tampa Mountain and discovered a cable car that was actually open and working, so up we went to the top of the mountain, well, hill really. It had great views of the whole of the town, so of course out came the cameras. We found a trail up to the flag post area, so Vicky clambered through the undergrowth, although there were no Japanese tourists to scare this time, unlike Moscow, and I duly documented the event photograph-wise.

When we came back down, there was more sightseeing around the town.

Later, as the rain started to fall, we went to find some food. We found a cosy bar/cafe and spent a pleasant hour there, eating and watching the world according to Brasov, go by. Each evening, back in our room, we would go through all of the photographs we had taken that day, erase those which were faulty in any way, or were repeats, the main editing to be done back in England; a mammoth task as you could imagine. We had some great talks about where we had been and what we had seen.

Day 63 June 24th

It was time to move on again. John came to take us to the station. It was like meeting up with an old friend, with goodbye hugs on the station steps. We got our tickets for Sighisaora but were unable to book seats. We soon saw why; the platform was absolutely packed, as was the train when it arrived. A platform worker told us to go up to the front carriage as we might have more chance of a seat, but no such luck, but we were able to sit on our cases in the doorway.

It seems that this was the day that the Capital's workers returned to their villages for their rest periods. After a while, with the gentle rocking of the train, I began to feel nauseous, first time during the whole trip. I rummaged through my luggage to find a plastic bag, just in case, and sat taking deep breaths while apparently my face became whiter and whiter, and then with a distinct green tinge. The young man nearest the doors asked me if I needed some air and began to open the doors to allow for some draught. The doors stayed open a little, and after we had pulled into a very small station, remained completely open. It was a bizarre situation, seated on a moving train, on my case, by wide open doors, just holding onto the hand rail. I loved it; my unwell feeling vanished and I couldn't help feeling that this would never have happened at home, there would been alarms going off everywhere. Thing was, I felt completely safe, and the other passengers didn't turn a hair.

The train wasn't a high-speed one as you must have guessed, so there was plenty of time to see the countryside rolling by, and beautiful it was too. The stations were all very small and the train gradually emptied out as the passengers got off at their respective villages. I never before saw so many people crossing the train tracks, as on this trip.

There was a family on the other side of the glass from Vicky and I and as soon as a seat became available, one of them came to get me. What nice people, a mother and her two adult sons. The two men, Atila and Bebe both spoke some English and were able to translate the conversation back to mum Margarite. Like others on the train, the men were returning home from their work in the capital. What a laugh I had with them; I think we put the world to rights in a mixture of languages, and lots of hand gestures. Poor Vicky still did not have a seat so was outside of this conversation group. Still, it wasn't too long before someone else got off and she was able to sit near us. I have to say, that older people are certainly respected in Eastern European cultures. I was sorry to see them get off at their village, but with hugs all round and a friendly wave from the train tracks, they were gone.

We carried on to our destination of Sighisaora. A city on the Tarnava Mare River, in Mures county, Transylvania.

'Urban status was granted in 1367. A fascinating medieval fortified city listed as a world heritage site. Reputedly the birthplace of Vlad Tepes in 1431, as his parents had lived in the city 1431 – 1435 whilst in exile.'

You could see the emblem of the Dragon everywhere you looked.

We booked into our hotel on the edge of the old town area, had a rest then went out for a stroll. We wandered around, took some photographs, what a place. Straight out of the middle ages, we just loved it.

We found the house where Vlad (the Impaler) had been born. Part of it was a restaurant, but up the stairs was a mock-up of a room complete with coffin and 'vampire' figure. It is strange that in places like that, even though I knew the props were not real, my mind started to play tricks, so I'm afraid I had to leave. I got thoroughly spooked trying to take a photo of Vicky, which for some reason just wouldn't be taken. That's it; I fled from the room and stood by a doorway waiting for her.

The guy in the coffin was perfectly still, but as Vicky came out, the poor man had a coughing fit, sitting bolt upright in the coffin. We all laughed, a little more loudly than was appropriate I thought. Funny what fear does to you. We decided to have our meal in the restaurant and managed to scare the waiter by telling him about our jobs; we both work for the Blood Service. I wasn't sure he believed us, but was too afraid not to believe. I finally managed to get a photograph of Vicky in the Restaurant.

When we came out it was twilight, so we took some very atmospheric photos, on the way back to the hotel. We decided that we liked Sighisaora very much.

Day 64

It was another sightseeing day. We went up the Clock Tower into a small museum with some strange artefacts, and were able to see the components of the revolving section, odd figures that intermittently appeared on the outside, under the clock face.

We were able to see some beautiful views over both the new and old parts of the town.

We saw a church up on the hill, so decided that would be our next venture. Up the side of the hill was a covered stairway, quite dark and eerie. We heard music coming from it and as we started up we saw it was a busker, an elderly woman in white, singing and playing the guitar.

It was very unsettling particularly as she said not a word, but just carried on strumming the very strange music. We did wonder just how real she was, so we were glad to get past her and relieved when we came out into the open at the top of the hill. There was a small school which we went into, then on to the church. We had a look around, then Vicky went outside whilst I braved the crypt.

When I came outside again, the local man at the entrance, who gave out the information sheets, stopped me. Once he had realised that I was English, he started to converse with me.

"Wait" he said, "I have a joke for you".

This will be good, I thought, *standing in a church porch way, listening to a joke*. Hmm, okay.

"So", he started off, "an old couple 50 years married, invite their newly married grand-relations for a meal. After a while the old man said to his wife 'light of my life, shall we have our starter now?' 'Of course, my darling' she replied. After more conversation the old man again turned to his wife and said 'star of my heaven, shall we have our main meal now?'. 'Oh yes, my beloved' she said. The young couple were impressed by the love and respect between the old couple especially after so many years married. 'love of my life, shall we have our dessert now?', and as before she smiled sweetly at him and brought the food. Later on over drinks, the two men were talking, the ladies elsewhere in the house. The young man said 'I cannot get over how affectionate you are after all of this time. I did not think it was possible to stay romantic after so many years'. 'Well', said the old man, 'I have forgotten her name, so what else could I say?'".

I laughed, he laughed and I thought to myself, *only in Romania, standing on the edge of a cemetery, in the birthplace of Vlad Dracul, listening to a joke in English.*

I liked it, and I very much liked those people, warm, friendly and very welcoming.

I met up with Vicky, who was, as she had been doing in the Moscow Novotnaya Cemetery, rummaging about in the undergrowth. I do worry about her sometimes. She was a sight to behold, bursting forth, wearing her dress with skulls on it, but then that was just her, and may she never change. I saw a strange looking bug on a plant; it reminded me of the pictures that I had seen of, as Vicky had put it, 'Vlad lad'.

We came back down to the town square, to be met with a downpour, got absolutely soaked, so we ducked into a small cafe for some sustenance. There was more sightseeing to be done once it cleared. We went into the large church opposite to where we were staying; it had a very impressive interior, then back to the hotel, a warm shower, meal, and bed.

Day 65

It was the last day in Romania, we had really enjoyed it, and we were sad to go. Unfortunately both Vicky and I were not well, colds and chesty coughs. The weather was atrocious and the thought of wandering around all day was very off-putting, as our onward train was not until 10 p.m. I spoke to the receptionist about hiring the room for another day, but explained that we would be leaving early evening. She had a word with her boss and the outcome was that they allowed us to stay in the room until 8 p.m., free of charge, and they were very sorry that we were not well. How amazing was that.

This gave us time to take our medication, rest and regain some energy for the move to Hungary. We slept on and off during the day, the rest of the time being spent staring out of the window. We watched the traffic coping with the rain; my word, we did see some sights.

We left the hotel feeling much better, went for a meal, then on to the station. Vicky had rescued a little bird, which she reluctantly had to leave behind, albeit in a safe place. The station was deserted.

It felt all a bit strange and foreboding, and we began to wonder if we had made a mistake about the time, but then another man arrived. We could hear dogs howling, Vicky was convinced they were wolves. Well, they may have been; this was Transylvania after all. The train arrived, much to our relief, and on time, so we clambered aboard, found our cabin for the overnight trip to Budapest. We were relieved to be tucked up for the night, but sad to have left Romania.

Chapter 15

Gina in Budapest, Hungary and Vienna, Austria.

I met Gina in the late 1990s when we both worked together at the National Blood Service. I liked her immediately, a gentle and very giving soul who it has been my pleasure to call Friend.

Vicky and I were still travelling companions, but this was where she would be leaving me for home, having first had a lightning tour of Budapest.

Day 66

'The capital city of Hungary, Budapest is one of the largest in Europe. After the unification of Buda and Pest in 1873 it became a single city occupying both banks of the River. It was originally a Celtic settlement, that endured nearly 150 years of Ottoman rule then after many changes of rule became a soviet satellite in 1956, in a violent takeover, and remained so until 1991. It is a world heritage site with examples of architecture from Roman, Gothic, Byzantine, Renaissance, Baroque, Art Nouveau and Contemporary. An important trade crossroads and major economic hub.'

We arrived at Keleti Station at a reasonable hour, put the luggage in a locker at the station, and then it was off to find some sustenance.

Once fed, we found a HoHo bus and spent the next few hours sightseeing. The day just flew by. We saw far more western influence in Hungary, in the buildings, the vehicles and the attitudes. As said, this was Vicky's last day with me and it was sad to see her go after nearly five weeks and four countries. I went to the airport to see her off, then went down to the Arrivals lounge to meet Gina, who was coming in on the plane that Vicky would be leaving on. Not that they saw each other, at least not until we all got home to England again.

So, it was time for the start of a new part of the adventure. We went back into the city, collected my luggage, and found our way to the Apart Hotel, which was in the 'arty' section of the city, lots of street cafes, restaurants, leafy avenues and a wonderful swirling of people on their way to who knows where.

We loved the apartment the moment we saw it. It was above the restaurants, through a very imposing door and in a block that looked like a 1940s film set. The lift had corrugated concertina doors opening out on to a balconied floor where the apartment was situated. We had a bedroom each, plus large sitting room, bathroom and kitchen. Loved it, loved it. We unpacked then went downstairs for a leisurely meal, a good catch up chat, then literally through the door behind us, and up to bed. I knew I was going to like it there.

Day 67

We woke up to the strains of a violin being played, so atmospheric and so fitting in that amazing old building. I felt so at home, a feeling that I had when I visited Hungary with my Mum and sister Christine some years earlier. In my ancestry somewhere, maybe. We had our breakfast in the flat then out for the day. You'll never guess what we did first, well yes of course, but a HoHo does help you get your bearings and give you a taste of the sights and sounds of the city. We did laugh because even the buses themselves were decorated with comic depictions of would-be passengers.

We went across the Chain Bridge to a vantage point where the city, on both sides of the river, could be seen. The route of the bus took us past a synagogue, purportedly the largest in Europe, and many decorated buildings both commercial and residential. In common with other European cities we saw many statues, both large and small depicting various historical events, including the Legacy Statue with its inscription 'to your Homeland, without fail, be faithful O Hungarian', and the site of the Mass carried out by Pope John Paul II.

A beautiful city of contrasts, with modern buildings in the newer sections, and at its heart a mix of old architectural styles. An efficient Tram service still ran, which added to the 'old-fashioned' feel of the place.

There was still evidence of Soviet Rule in some buildings, such as the Headquarters of the Secret Police, and we saw a street exhibition depicting the Iron Curtain era and information boards referencing the years between 1962 and 1989. I took lots of photographs - does that surprise you? Of course not. It was very hot, we even got a little sunburnt.

After the bus trip, we decided to travel by boat down the river, which was the Danube, immortalised by Strauss in his famous waltz. We saw some of the most amazing buildings I had ever seen; Buda Castle, Mattias Church, the Fishermen's Bastion, and the Parliament building, so naturally many more photographs.

We spent the whole day travelling around, then found a park to wander through, a lovely restful oasis in the middle of the city.

We also found the Hard Rock Cafe. Great places, and not too expensive, which at that end of the trip really mattered, so for lunch we came.

We visited Heroes square, a large open area that was known for its statue complex.

'This included depictions of the seven chiefdoms of the Magyars, the tomb of the unknown soldier and statues of other iconic leaders. The sculptures were made by Zala Gyorgy. The central feature was begun in 1896 to commemorate the 100th anniversary of the Hungarian conquest and the subsequent foundation of the Hungarian state. The central feature is the Millennium memorial, and other statues include Stephen I and Charles I of Hungary, the couple of Labour and Wealth, symbol of War, also Female statue of Peace, Matthew Coronavirus and Lajos Kossuth.'

After a very full day, it was back to our apartment, a quick shower and change. In those surroundings we again felt we had to dress up for dinner. Then down to the restaurant for our evening meal. It was really nice to eat outside, and as this was the Andrassy quarter, the whole street was filled with tables and chairs outside each of the eateries.

Again, it was very interesting to hear the hubbub of voices in many languages. We only had to go back through the door to our apartment block, so no worry about getting home, and no taxis. Once back in our 'home', we sat and reminisced about our day, and what to do on the next one. Gina, as was the case with my other friends, was very good company, so it was enjoyable to unwind before bed.

Day 68

We had a lovely cultural day and walked along a wide tree lined road, up to the Art Gallery. There was an amazing Art collection within, so many old masters on show, plus a large collection of Toulouse Lautrec paintings. We were only allowed to photograph certain things, and then without flash; that was fair enough as the flash damaged the pictures, but it was amazing how many people ignored that request.

We wandered back to the Opera House where we had booked a tour. What a beautiful golden palace, we were taken around various areas, great photographic opportunities, although sometimes we just stood and soaked up the atmosphere. We went through a gallery that showed paintings of previous singers and actors and were then treated to a short recital with one of the present cast who sang an aria for us. A very pleasant experience all around. On the way home we passed a wonderful looking shop with cakes and pastries that just had to be tried. We chose one each and took our treats back to the apartment where we sat in the opulent, well in our eyes, splendour of our lounge, with a cup of tea and our gorgeous cakes. A fitting experience after our cultural day. We had our evening meal at the Restaurant 'Circus', and later wandered around the area for an evening stroll. It was a really lovely day, I enjoyed every minute of it.

Day 69 June 30th

It was another moving day, this time off to Vienna, Austria. We had a good journey, good clean train as expected, and arrived in Vienna about 2 p.m.

'The capital and largest city in Austria, said to be 'The city of Dreams' because it was home to Sigmund Freud, the world's first Psycho-Analyst. Evidence of continuous habitation since 500BC. In 1440 it became the

resident city of the Hapsburg Dynasty and later the capital of the Austro-Hungarian Empire. During WWII Austria ceased to exist in its own right, becoming part of Germany, but regained its sovereignty in 1955. The city has been home to many musical luminaries including Mozart, Hayden, Beethoven, Schubert, Brahms, Mahler, Strauss, Salieri and Liszt amongst others. There are many major tourist attractions including Palaces Hofburg and Schonbrunn which is also home to the world's oldest Zoo. The Vienna Boys Choir and the Lippizanes horses at the Spanish School. The city is also the location of a number of United Nations offices.'

We took a taxi to the hotel, another Apart Hotel, again another lovely apartment. Smaller than the Budapest apartment, but it was just as interesting in its own way. One thing about the trip; I had stayed in very many different places, from shady one-roomed bedsits, to flats, a small Chinese house, a boat and some quite luxurious hotels. I loved them all, loved the quirkiness of them, the different feel of them being suited to the country in which they were situated.

We unpacked and went for a walk. We spent some time in the coolness of St. Peter's Church, which was far more ornate than some of the other churches I had seen of late. We found a lovely cafe, so of course it was time for 'coffee and cake', a concept that my friend Karen had introduced me to many years before, which I, and another friend, Adrienne, had adopted with gusto. If you thought that a lot of the trip was spent eating, you would be right Well, we had to try out the local eateries. We stayed pretty much in the local area, then went back to our 'home', showered and out for our evening meal.

Day 70

After a good sleep, we made ready and then went out. HoHo buses here we come. There were so many beautiful buildings and spaces to look at, for instance the Parliament Building with its decorative pillars and gargantuan statue of Pallas Athene:

The Hapsburg Palace and Gardens complete with the Mozart statue:

and the Opera House. We also saw the not quite so beautiful residential areas. However I liked the contrast in architecture so consequently took a lot of photographs. A number of the buildings had art on them, interesting drawings, and at the other end of the scale, a lot of graffiti too, although some of it was just as valid art, I thought anyway.

As in keeping with many other European cities, there were a large number of commemorative statues. On one of the shopping streets there were a series of plaques that celebrated various famous people, laid into the pavement, like those outside of the Chinese Theatre in Los Angeles.

Another city of contrasts, but all the more interesting for it. We had a laugh on the bus, as we tried to catch our reflections in the windows of the buildings we passed. Like Budapest, Vienna also has a Tram system that rumbled through the streets.

We went out to the Schonbrunn Castle, what a place it was, the beautiful summer home of the Hapsburgs.

We learnt about Kaiser Frans Joseph I and his beautiful wife Elizabeth known as Sisi. We heard how court life would have been, but for all of the luxury I felt that it must have been very claustrophobic. We wandered through the Palace, the courtyards and the gardens, then a visit to the gift shop completed our visit. We took the bus back into the city and continued our tour getting off to see again the Cathedral of St. Stephen, with it's heavy ornamentation of wood, paintings and gold.

The days were just not long enough when there was so much to see. Sadly it rained most of the day, but hey ho. Back on the bus we crossed the River Danube to an area where one of the oldest, if not THE oldest Ferris Wheel in Europe was situated.

A fascinating city of contrasts, as said. We were now hungry, so it was back to get ready to go out for our evening meal

Day 71

We had an early start; we were off to Salzburg, just for the day. A good journey, with beautiful scenery as we crossed Austria, east to west. The houses looked just as you would have imagined them to look, 'chocolate box' images. A pleasant trip, on a clean and comfortable train. We arrived, and went for a coffee/tea break to spike up our energy levels for the day ahead. We found the HoHos and went for our customary first look, to get our bearings. Well, what a place, absolutely stunning, I kept wanting to burst into song, you know the ones, but thankfully, for everyone's sake, I resisted the urge.

We had a walk around the immediate area, saw the guides in their national costumes, and even the odd living statue, then decided to go up to the fortress, using the monorail system. It was very steep, which I loved, taking pictures from the front window of the little carriage. Gina, however was not so enamoured, but I was so proud of her conquering her height fears, firstly by going up, staying at the top for a while and then standing with me at the front on the way down. It was quite something to see someone override their fears and to actually enjoy the resulting victory, for instance, by being able to take photographs over parapets. Well done Gina.

The view from the top was absolutely stunning:

As if there was ever any doubt.

We spent some time in a lovely cafe, drinking hot chocolate, and looking at the amazing views, the mountains in the distance, the high hills where the lonely goat herders may have stood, oops, another song coming on. Deep breaths. Also the houses and parkland below us. Beautiful clear air to breathe in, it was an incredible experience.

We walked further around the cliff top to the Nonnberg Abbey, the Nunnery where the real Maria (later von Trapp), had been a novice Nun. The Nunnery was private, but the church was open for all. It was suggested that we wait there for a while as the Nuns were due to sing their devotions. The place was very calming, so after looking around, we just sat in contemplation. Within minutes, the church was filled with the most beautiful singing, which swirled gently around the building until it filled not only us, but the whole space. The Nuns were in an upstairs chamber so sadly we did not see them, but it was enough just to hear them. We sat, not speaking for quite some time afterwards.

We wandered back down to the main street and sat in Mirabell Park for a while and enjoyed the sunshine, then walked along to see the house of Mozart's birth. We also went to the cathedral, where we took in all of the sights, which included a magnificent organ, as we quietly sat in the coolness of the interior. There was such a lot to see in one day and a lot we did see, including the Liechtenstein Garden Palace and a beautiful view across a lake where stood the house used as the von Trapp mansion in the film, whose songs we knew so well. The house was now privately owned, so no visiting. Sadly it was time to go back to the train, meal and bed. I could not believe that the next day was going to be Gina's last one; we had had a lovely time. The time spent with each friend had been really good and very different, it was a privilege.

Day 72

It was moving day again. Just time for a little more sightseeing around the area where we have been staying, then it was off to the airport with Gina. She was going home and I was going to the Czech Republic by overnight train, to meet up with my next companion. We had a little drama on the way to the airport; there were horrendous queues and stoppages, so eventually our coach, plus other airport coaches drove up the wide hard shoulder on the link road. We got the impression that this happened often. Gina only just made her plane and of course it was a bit hairy for me to get back for my train. Nothing like a bit of drama to get the Adrenaline going. It was a good journey once I had calmed down.

I was originally going to break my journey at Bryn, but decided to go straight through to Prague. Luckily I was able to let the hotel at Bryn know, wonderful mobile phones. I arrived at the main station after 11 p.m. and immediately got embroiled in a row with, you've guessed it, taxi drivers. I was furious that they wanted to charge me almost the same money to go a short distance, that my ticket from Vienna had cost me. After much shouting - in my defence I was tired and had, I believed, good cause, I had to give in. It was very late and I had no choice as I didn't know where the hotel was located. When I got there, even they told me I had been ripped off. Ah well, to bed.

Chapter 16

Liz in the Czech Republic and Germany

A fellow lover of travel and adventure, from my home area of the Wirral. Involved with many projects, and like me, a Hard Rock cafe enthusiast.

Day 73

I slept most of the morning, and was on my own as my next adventurer would not arrive for another two days. Once washed, dressed and fed, it was time to go exploring. I had been to Prague once before, with Linda, but it was in February and the city had a completely different look with the snow and everyone bundled up in their winter clothes, protection against the minus 11°C temperature. However this was July 5th, and the sun shone brightly. I walked down to Wencelas Square.

This was now the centre of the business and cultural communities in the new part of Prague. It was once a traditional setting for public gatherings, celebrations and demonstrations such as the ones in 1945 and 1969, and lastly during the 'Velvet Revolution' in 1989. The Square was named after the Saint Wencelas, patron saint of Bohemia. The north western edge of the Square ran against the border of the new and old town.

I spent the day sightseeing, took lots of photos, found a nice cafe, then it was back to the hotel, just ahead of an absolute downpour. A beautiful city with architecture from the Gothic, Renaissance and Baroque eras. I had a restful evening reflecting on everything I had seen and experienced thus far, and the adventures that were still to come.

Day 74

I moved on to the hotel that I had booked, ready for the arrival of my next fellow traveller. This hotel was nearer to the old town section. I settled in, unpacked, dab hand at this moving manoeuvre now, fed and went out again late afternoon. I found a sightseeing tour, in a large open topped car, that went around various locations in the city. I was sharing this with a group of six British women, who studiously ignored me and just chatted amongst themselves even after I had said "hello". I didn't mind them not talking, but a hello would have been nice. Ah well, not like anywhere else I had been to, where regardless of nationality, people were polite. Still, I had plenty to occupy myself with, and took many, many photographs. I found a nice restaurant later, in the Ambassador Hotel and had my evening meal. It was very good, but far too much. The waiters were very attentive as I was on my own. Following the downpour of yesterday, the weather was very hot, although nothing like the temperatures in China. Back for the night, I had a good sleep ready for the trip to the airport to meet my next companion.

Day 75 July 7th

I spent the morning around the hotel, then once outside found a small park, sat down and promptly fell asleep - oops, obviously I felt very relaxed. I had a good journey out to the airport, met up with my friend and returned to the hotel with no incidents. We had a rest, then went out for our evening meal. We found a tavern-style restaurant very close to our hotel and spent an enjoyable first evening.

Day 76

We went for a mooch around the city, starting with Wencelas Square. As said, once the site of rallies, and even violent clashes, the area now had benches, stalls and greenery, no more big gatherings there then. We went to see the memorial to Jan Palach, a student who set himself alight in protest against the communist takeover of the country.

Again history coming to life as this was an occurrence that had taken place during my lifetime. There was a band there singing protest songs, an amazing sight given the history of the place.

The boulevard leading down to the old town, had many beautiful buildings, such as the Hotel Europa, and we found, much to our amusement a cafe/bar that served the drinks in a very unique way.

There were several miniature trains running around a track which surrounded the whole cafe. You placed your drinks order and the train brought it to your table. But you must not be too long retrieving them, as the train moved on quite quickly. Great fun.

I spoke to my family on the phone, as I had done every Tuesday since I had started my trip. It was good and necessary to keep in touch. I just had to watch the time zone differences in some of the countries visited; in my enthusiasm I had phoned Mum in the middle of the night, and given her quite a fright.

It was very hot again. My friend had found a craft shop on-line and wanted to visit it. We eventually found it after a long walk up behind the St. Ludmilla church. There was some sort of art exhibition going on in the area, market style stalls and even a busker who played Jazz music.

There was also a dance festival with dancers from Romania. I loved the Romanian leg of this trip, so I felt quite nostalgic. Items having been bought, we went for a wander around the church, it was very ornate as you can imagine. Next stop was afternoon tea. We found a really nice little cafe with delicious home-made cakes. We had a chat with the owner, most pleasant, then it was time to walk back into the city area.

Back in the old town we went to the main square, saw the amazing Astronomical Clock, first installed in 1410 and which had three main sections: the astronomical dial in the form of a primitive planetarium, the 'walk of the Apostles' and other sculptures and the Calendar dial. The clock had been renovated many times through the centuries, the last time being 2005.

We also saw the crosses in the pavement depicting the execution of 27 Knights of the city, leaders of the Bohemian Revolt.

'A Protestant uprising against the Catholic Hapsburgs, that had resulted in the Thirty Years War and eventual defeat in 1620 after the Battle of the White Mountain. This was followed by harsh large scale re-catholicisation of the Country.'

A memorial stone listed the names of those executed. We stood in awe of the beautiful church Our Lady of Tyn, a dominant feature of the square since the 14th Century, where renovations both inside and out had been taking place since 1973.

We had our evening meal and a rest before it was time to go out on an arranged walking tour to underground areas of Prague. An absolute downpour, again, but luckily we were sheltered for most of the time. Our guide was Karel, a young man but very knowledgeable. He showed us sunken houses; in the past the street levels had been raised because of flooding by the River Vitava. It was a late night but interesting for all of that. I had a good sleep which was just as well as we had a busy day coming up.

Day 77

We went on the Ultimate Tour, a six hour tour involving walking, boat and tram. Firstly we met up with fellow 'tourers', all of different nationalities, but again with English as the common language. So, off we went, firstly around the old town then across the Charles Bridge. High on a hill we could see the Metronome Sculpture, crafted in 1991, that had replaced the original Stalin Statue, that stood there during the Soviet period.

'The Charles Bridge was started in 1357 and finished at the beginning of the 15*th* century. It replaced the old Judith Bridge that was damaged in a flood in 1342. It was named 'The Charles Bridge' in 1870, previously referred to as 'The Stone Bridge'. It is a bow bridge protected by ice guards and decorated by 30 statues along its length. Originally used by vehicular traffic, but pedestrianised since 1978. The statues are mainly saints and patron saints and include St. Luthgard and John of Nepomuk. It is thought to be good luck to rub some of the statues.'

We went along the river's edge to join a small boat, whereby we sailed down the river, and eventually arrived at a pre-selected restaurant. En-route we learnt about the carvings on the various bridges which, legend had it, were there to warn off would-be attackers of the city, and were associated with many stories involving sailors on the river.

After our food, we had an exciting trip on a tram, up to the castle. Exciting because it was a scramble for all of us to get on; the trams certainly do not dawdle at the stops. I don't think that our guide, called Nina by the way, was the worrying type, the assumption being that we would all make it on to the transport, or it would be a long slog up the hill.

The castle was interesting, as castles are, with its varied history in war times and in peace. We also got to see the changing of the guard. Later we stood at a viewing area, overlooking small vineyards, and through them to the City spread out before us, the old and new areas and the river meandering through the scene, glinting in the sun.

Suddenly the six hours were over, and I have to say, it went very quickly. Our guide was excellent, and we spent some time with her on our own, whilst we walked back down the hill to the tram stop, for the journey back into the old town. A fun-filled busy day.

To finish things off, and also because we were hungry again, all that fresh air, we went to the Hard Rock Cafe for our tea meal. We met a great waiter who served us and then arranged with another guy to take us on an individual tour of the building. He was an Australian, with a great sense of humour. We just loved the tour, very rock and roll. I found that wherever I was, people were happy to give you their time and knowledge. We came back to the hotel, watched a DVD, then bed. Exhausted but happy.

Day 78 July 10th

We were out early, time seemed to gallop by when there was so much to see and do, and then ran out before you had done the half of it. We went to a Communism Museum, it was very interesting and informative, if not a little scary. As I had found when I visited Berlin, the myth put forward about life in the communist era, happy people, shops full of goods, was very different to the reality, especially knowing you were under surveillance all of the time, and not knowing who to trust. How fortunate are we to be able to say what we want, be what we want and go where we want.

We went on another walking tour, I was fitter then, around the Communist sites, saw the 1989 end of Communism plaque and various other historical places, buildings such as the Secret Police H.Q. and the locations of various other incidents.

This culminated with another tram ride - I just loved those rides - up to a Nuclear Bunker, where we saw, put on and generally had fun with the uniforms, gas masks and weapons. No lights out like the Moscow bunker, thankfully.

We came back into the old town, had a rest in the hotel before going out for our evening meal. A German rock band was playing in the square, so we stood with many others, locals and tourists, enjoying the music until hunger got the better of us. Later back at the hotel, we packed ready to move on to Cologne the next day.

Day 79

We were going on the overnight sleeper train. Oh, what was it with German sleeper trains? The carriages were not being attached until we reached Berlin, about midnight. It was a pain having to move all the luggage several times. They seemed determined not to let you get a good night's sleep. Still, that was for later. We had the rest of the day to fill first. We had decided to take a trip to the Terezin Concentration camp.

'*A former military fortress comprising a citadel and walled garrison town. Following the occupation of Czech lands by Nazi Germany, Terezin was adapted to a ghetto and concentration camp. Not for extermination, however about 33,000 died due to the appalling conditions. The camp was closed in 1948.*'

It was a fascinating trip, very informative. It really brought things home to us. There was an eerie heavy silence there broken only by the occasional click of camera shutters. Outside was a beautifully laid out Jewish cemetery, which was shocking in the numbers of graves that were there.

Back in the town, we had a drink whilst waiting for the coach. We had no appetite for eating.

So back to the train; we travelled the first section of the trip with a young man called Tomas who was on his way to visit his girlfriend in

Germany, in what was originally in East Germany. We had a good laugh with him, especially when we told him about photographs and jumping trees. Everyone had been sceptical about the phenomenon at first, but soon learnt when trying to capture views of the countryside from the train. A pleasant journey which we then continued to Berlin for our change-over to our sleeping cabin.

The cabin had six bunks, so we spent a very cosy night with two Dutch lads, a Polish lady and her husband and my friend and I. Gone were the days of the first-class cabins, the money was much tighter now. To be fair, the journey was much better than I had feared. We all awoke in the morning, with activity from the Polish guy who rummaged in his case, then produced a bottle of Vodka, which he then proceeded to share with everyone. Oh, much too early in the day for me, the sun wasn't even up, but how very Eastern European. They were all very nice sharing people; we laughed and went our separate ways having reached Cologne.

Day 80

The sight of the Cathedral, which sits on the doorstep of the station, was just as impressive as it had been the first time I was there. We both appreciated its splendid facade. We had breakfast at the station, then took a taxi to the hotel. The hotel, to our amusement, nestled between two sex-shops, in what looked to be a pretty seedy area. So first impression, not good, but as with all things, we soon adjusted to our surroundings. We unpacked, rested then went off to find, oh yes, you've guessed it, the HoHo buses.

We arrived back at the Cathedral in time to see the inauguration of the new Archbishop. The building was full, standing room only, and the service was carried out with the expected pomp and ceremony, yet another experience for us to enjoy.

Then there was more walking about the old town area. I acted as a guide once again and showed off the lovely hotel that I had stayed in originally, down on the banks of the Rhine. Then it was back to our new hotel for a rest before our evening meal. We went again to the Hard Rock cafe, I just loved these places. Our waiter was an English guy, a good bloke, interesting, funny and friendly. I told him of my other HRC visits in the various countries. It was a most enjoyable evening. I was so tired, but fortunately had a really good sleep.

Day 81 July 13th

I woke up refreshed, we had a good breakfast, then it was down to the terminal for the Rhine River Cruise.

We sat on the top deck, chatting, drinking tea/coffee and just generally surveying the scenery, which was different to what we had seen in the Czech Republic.

Each place I had visited had its own sights, smells, sounds and charm, so much to see but sadly I could really only get a flavour of each due to time constraints. Later we wandered around the city. There was a 10km race taking place, so we followed the competitors to the finish line in a small park area.

We walked through the main shopping area and later found the 4711 Eau de Cologne parent shop. We peered through the window at the racks of bottles, some that dated from the 18th Century when the fragrance was first created by Johann Maria Farina.

Thankfully, as it was a Sunday, it was closed. It could have been a very expensive experience. We found a nice inn for lunch.

All too soon it was time to go back to the hotel for the luggage, then out to the airport for a parting of the ways. I was moving on to London the next day, courtesy of the Eurostar, so I still had another night in Germany. When I arrived back, there were crowds of people at the station, dressed in Germany's flag colours; even the shop windows were decorated.

I wondered what was going on. Explanation, it was the World Cup football match between Germany and Brazil. I grabbed a sandwich at the station then went back to the room for the evening. Must say, I also watched the Match on my TV. The window was open so I could hear talking, shouting, and cheering from all around the area. Germany won, so imagine the noise.

Chapter 17

Linda in London

I have known Linda since the early 1980s, firstly as a work colleague when we worked together in the Youth Information Bureau, Birkenhead, and then, sharing many holidays, good happy times and some sad times, in other words, as a good friend.

Day 82

It was another moving day, this time to London to meet Linda. I went by train from Cologne to Brussels for the first leg of the journey. I had a reflective time; staring out of the window, I couldn't quite believe that my trip was almost at an end, but what memories I had stored up, as well as hundreds of photographs. Still, one more place to visit, and another friend to meet, before home.

I had to wait about three hours for the Eurostar/London connection. It was a good journey; I got talking to a guy in the next seat, so we shared holiday reminiscences.

I walked to the Hotel, about 400 yards from the station. It hardly seemed to have been any time from when I walked along with Simon and Penny on the outward journey, dragging all my heavy luggage, but with a well of excitement within me, which was still there, I must add.

Linda was already there, so we had a cup of tea. I unpacked then luxuriated in the bath - heaven. Later we walked down to Covent Garden, and would you believe, took more photographs.

'This well known and much visited part of London is situated in the Westminster area, on the fringes of the West End. A former fruit and Vegetable market, dating back to 1654. However by the 18th century it

had become part of the 'Red Light' district. It reopened as a retail market in 1979. The area now has over sixty pubs and bars, a wide range of Restaurants, amongst which is Rules, the oldest in London, established in 1798.'

Linda and I had already decided that we were going to treat this the same as any other leg of the journey. We were solely tourists seeing London for the first time, even though we had both been many times in the past. It was fun to try to see things through fresh eyes. Also how we were treated was different; speaking of which, we found people most helpful, even, dare I say it, taxi drivers. We had our evening meal at a Turkish Restaurant just around the corner from the hotel. It was a huge meal; we both have really good appetites but this left us both defeated. A slow walk back, chatting all the way. It was good to meet up. Good night's sleep.

Day 83

We surfaced early (ish). We got ourselves ready then straight out for, oh yes, the HoHo buses. This was most definitely the best way to get your bearings in a new place. So many cities had bought into the idea, perfect for tourists. I always liked to complete the whole trip first, to gain some knowledge of the area, so that I would know where to stop off on the second time around. A little like life, I suppose; gather the information first, then pick and choose. We went on a Blue Line bus, a good long trip around London. There was so much to see, also with a good commentary, so we learnt a lot.

We passed Baker Street, saw the Sherlock Holmes statue, Eros, St. Paul's Cathedral and Westminster Abbey.

We also went through the business centre of London, with its signature dragon statue, standing proud.

We also saw new iconic buildings such as the Gherkin and the Shard. We were treated to a detachment of Guards in full regalia riding through the streets. We saw Oliver Cromwell, in cast bronze, standing outside the Houses of Parliament and of course Big Ben, the nickname given to the Great Bell in the Clock Tower of the Palace of Westminster, completed in 1859.

We travelled through other areas such as Marble Arch, Downing Street, not forgetting Trafalgar Square, The Embankment, and caught sight of the London Eye. We did not ride on it but I had done so in the past, and enjoyed the amazing views over London.

Then out to Hyde Park and the leafy suburbs of Chelsea. There were many, many famous sights, too numerous to mention. We drank them all in, the poor camera shutter went into overdrive.

We got off at Harrods, had a quick wander around, especially the Food Hall, Linda being a good cook was especially interested.

We each bought a sandwich each and sat on a bench outside. We just watched the world go by, and believe me the world and his and her relatives certainly did go by. I saw people representative of everywhere I had travelled to, during my trip.

Back on the bus, we went to the Tower of London.

'An historic castle on the north bank of the River Thames. Founded towards the end of 1066, the White Tower being built in 1078.

'It was at one time used as a royal residence, but in Tudor times, mainly as a prison, with notable prisoners such as Anne Boleyn and Sir Walter Rayleigh. It has long since been a tourist attraction housing the Crown Jewels, magnificent symbols of pomp and majesty, including the Crown used in the investiture of the monarchs of England.'

We also saw some of the more infamous locations within the tower grounds, such as Traitor's Gate, built by Edward I. At its most notorious in Tudor times, prisoners were brought by barge, along the Thames, some never to see freedom again.

And of course, this was the home of the famous Ravens.

I chatted with a resident, a Beefeater, resplendent in his red-adorned coat, who was very friendly, imparting his knowledge of the various sections of the Tower. Beefeaters historically were the Yeoman Warders of Her Majesty's Royal Palace and Fortress, known as The Tower of London. They are ceremonial guardians who have all been former Armed Forces members with at least 22 years service. Formed in 1485 by Henry VII, they wear the Heraldic Badge of the dynasty, the Tudor Rose. One of the warders traditionally had responsibility for the aforementioned Ravens who are said to have been in residence since the time of King Charles II. It has been said that 'if the Ravens should ever leave, the White Tower will fall, and disaster will befall the Kingdom'.

We decided to take a boat trip back down the Thames, whereupon one of the boat workers took it upon himself to give a running commentary, and very good it was too. Looking along the river, we saw the City of London skyline in one direction, and Westminster, in the other.

We also saw Cleopatra's Needle, The Globe Theatre (Elizabethan Playhouse associated with William Shakespeare, originally built in 1599, demolished in 1644, then rebuilt, the modern reconstruction opening in 1997), and the Millenium Bridge. We took a taxi back to the hotel, again a friendly helpful guy, who gave us some idea of the various sights that we were passing, and a reasonable price too.

One of the places we passed was the Hard Rock Cafe.

'The first of these was opened back in 1971, under the ownership of Americans Pete Morgan and Isaac Tigrett. By 1979 rock and roll memorabilia began covering the walls, a tradition which spread to others in the chain. As of 2015 there were 191 Hard Rock locations in 59 countries including 168 cafes, 23 hotels and 11 casinos. Legend has it that the music memorabilia began with an un-signed Fender Guitar from regular customer Eric Clapton, who used the Guitar to lay claim to a

specific seat. This gesture was followed by Pete Townsend, and now the Hard Rock archive includes over 77,000 items and is the largest private collection of 'Rock and Roll' memorabilia in the world.'

We had a rest then out for our last evening meal. Again, the portions were far too big. I was sorry to waste so much food, especially after having seen some of the sights and places that I had been to; it made me feel very uncomfortable. Also, I have since felt much more aware, and tried to use only what I have actually needed, and not just what I wanted. A world of difference. Back at the hotel, we had a long conversation before settling down, looked through all of the photos, and thought about tomorrow, another moving day, but this time it was the last one.

Day 84 July 16th

Well, this was it, homecoming day. Up early, it was 7 a.m. and I was showered, hair done and packed. The train wasn't until 13.00 but we both wanted to have a leisurely morning. A myriad of thoughts ran through my head. Now that the day had finally arrived, I was ready to go home to see everyone, my sons, Mum, sisters, other friends who had not been able to come, and of course my much loved Cairo Lancy.

We arrived at Lime Street Station, the mainline Liverpool station. An imposing edifice originally built in 1833 and which had undergone various revamps since.

I was pleased to see it. One more train ride left, the Underground to Wirral, Hamilton Square, taxi and home.

HOME

I let myself in and immediately Cairo was there to greet me. Paula said hello and Penny and Simon called after work. All safe and sound; I made many phone calls, it was 'business as usual'.

Wow, what a time I have had, absolutely drenched in memories.

How absolutely happy am I.

Chapter 18

AFTERWARDS

As promised, we all had a get-together in my house, my zen place, in the September. It was a very special night.

The photographs had all been printed and there was an album dedicated to each location. Those who came introduced themselves by name and by which Country/Countries they had visited.

It was fun and interesting, particularly as some of the people did not know each other as they were from different times and areas of my life.

The albums were distributed around the room for all to see. Paula made us lots of lovely food. I was especially grateful to her as she had looked after my Cairo, my house and now, our bellies.

A trip of a lifetime.

THANK YOU TO EVERYONE, HOWEVER INVOLVED.
YOU COULD NEVER BUY FRIENDSHIPS LIKE THESE.

Nina xxx

Appendix

FORMS OF TRANSPORT

TRAINS (Outward)
Virgin: U.K. - Liverpool Lime Street to London Euston
Eurostar: U.K. - St. Pancras to Brussels Midi BELGIUM
DB Bahn: Belgium - Brussels Midi to Cologne GERMANY
DB Bahn: Germany - Cologne to Copenhagen DENMARK
SJ AB: Sweden - Malmo to Gothenburg (plus day trips)
SJ AB: Sweden - Stockholm to Malmo via Karlstad
DB Bahn: Transit - Cologne to Warsaw POLAND
Krasnaya Strela: RUSSIA - Moscow to St. Petersburg/return Moscow
Trans Siberian: Russia – Moscow - Mongolia - Beijing CHINA
(Train 0034)
Bullet Trains: China - To Xi'an and Shanghai

(Inward)

Trans Manchurian: China - Beijing to Moscow RUSSIA
CFR: ROMANIA - Bucharest, Brasov, Sigisaora
CFR: Romania- Sighisaora to Budapest HUNGARY
MAV: Hungary - Budapest to Vienna AUSTRIA
OBB: Austria - Vienna to Salzburg
OBB: Austria - Vienna to Prague CZECH REPUBLIC
DB Bahn: Czech Republic - Prague to Cologne GERMANY
DB Bahn: Germany - Cologne to Brussels BELGIUM
Eurostar: Belgium - Brussels to London U.K.
Virgin: U.K. - London to Liverpool U.K.
Merseyrail: Home to the Wirral

METRO and UNDERGROUND
BELGIUM - Brussels to Antwerp
UNDERGROUND
DENMARK - around Copenhagen
SWEDEN - Stockholm to Airport
POLAND - Warsaw to Airport
RUSSIA - Airport, various trips around Moscow
CHINA - Airport, to Beijing West
U.K. - Liverpool to Wirral (Birkenhead)

PLANES
SAS Sweden: Internal - Gothenburg to Kiruna, via Stockholm
SAS Sweden: Internal - Kiruna to Stockholm
Aeroflot: POLAND - Warsaw to Moscow RUSSIA
Aeroflot: Russia - Moscow to Bucharest ROMANIA

BOATS
Harbour Cruise: DENMARK - Copenhagen
Harbour Cruise: SWEDEN - Stockholm
Ferry: SWEDEN - Stockholm Harbour to Skanzen
River Cruise: RUSSIA - St. Petersburg - Canals and River Neva
River Cruise: RUSSIA - Moscow - Moskva River
Lake Crossing: CHINA - Beijing to Summer Palace - Dragon Boat
River Cruise: GERMANY - River Rhine
River Cruise: U.K. - River Thames

OTHER FORMS OF TRANSPORT
Buses (HoHos): EVERY CITY
Buses (Intercity):
CHINA - Hangzhou to Huang Shan
CHINA - Huang Shan to Shanghai

Cable Cars:
AUSTRIA - Salzburg
CHINA - Great Wall, Yellow Mountains

GERMANY - Cologne
ROMANIA - Brasov

Husky Dog Team: SWEDEN - Kiruna
Rickshaws: CHINA - various, Beijing
Sightseeing Car: CZECH REPUBLIC - Prague

Small Tourist Trains:
GERMANY - Cologne - Zoo Express
SWEDEN - Karlstad - Marieborg Skogen
POLAND - City Tour

Taxis: MOST CITIES

Toboggan Run: CHINA - Great Wall at Mu Tian Yu

Trams: MOST CITIES

HOTELS/HOSTELS/HOMES from HOME
BELGIUM:
BnB Alegria
Spoorstraat 19
Antwerp
GERMANY (Outwards)
Lowenbrau Hotel
Frankenwerft 21
Cologne 50667
GERMANY (Inwards)
Hotel Novum Ahl Meerkatzen
Mathiasstr. 21
Alt Stadt, Cologne
DENMARK
Ansgar Hotel
Park Inn
B. Radisson

Engevj, Copenhagen 2300
SWEDEN
Hotel Vinter Palast
Kiruna
Anedin Hostel
Skeppsbron, Tillhusi
Gamelstan, Stockholm 1130
Savoy Hotel
Karlstad
Hotel Jorgan Koch, Malmo
POLAND
Apartment
Old Town Square
Rynek Starego Miastra 25
Warsaw
Hampton by Hilton
17 Stycznia 39F Street 1
Warsaw

RUSSIA
St. Petersburg
Hotel 3 Mosta
Moyka Emb.3
Moscow (Outward)
Apartment
Zamoryonova Street, Building 40,
District Yannu 1905
Moscow (Inward)
Basilica Hotel
Serebryanichesky Pereulok 1a
Tagansky, Moscow 101000
CHINA
Apartment. (J & C)
Qihelou South Alley, Qihelou Street
Dongcheng District

Beijing 100006
Huangshan Pine Ridge Lodge
Scenic area south gate
Huangshan, Tangkou 245800
G-Luxe Hangqiao S'hai
No. 1385 Huqingping Road
Shanghai 201702
ROMANIA
Bucharest
Zava Boutique Hotel
Stephan Mihaileanu 21
Bucharest 024021
Brasov
Pensiunea Casa Tepes
Str. Vlad Tepes 14
Brasov 500092
Sighisaora
Pensiunea San Gennaro Centru
Consiliul Europei Nr. 3, Sighisaora 545400
HUNGARY
Karma Boutique Apartments
Liszt Ferenc Square 11
1061 Budapest
AUSTRIA
Hotel am Brilliantemgrund
Bandgasse 4, 0.7 Neubau
1070 Vienna
CZECH REPUBLIC
Hotel Brixen
Soholska 44, Prague 02
Hotel U Suteru
Palackeho 72214
Prague 01
GREAT BRITAIN
Hotel Tavistock: Tavistock Square London WC1H 9EU

INDEX

A
Adrienne, 251
Aeroflot, 59, 205
Agriculture, 181
Alexander Gardens, 88, 93, 201
Angel, 119–120
Antwerp, 1–4, 10
Archbishop, 278
Army, 145, 186, 192
Art Gallery, 35, 250
Astronaut, 119
Astronomical Clocks, 44, 267
Atila, Bebe and Mum, 224
Atlas, 163
Aurora, 73
Austria, 241, 250–251, 256

B
Baby, 91, 155
Baikal, 97, 109, 185
Barabinsk, 106
Basilica St. Basils, 92
Beefeaters, 295
Beers and Bars, 6, 287
Beijing, 95, 97, 107, 115, 125, 127, 129, 131, 135, 143, 148–149, 153–154, 159, 163, 165, 169, 176, 180, 191
Belgium, 1–3
Bicycles, 4, 165
Big Ben, 290
Birkenhead, 26, 61, 72, 121, 285
Black Church, 219
Boats, 72

Bolotnaya Square, 94
Bolshoi, 89
Border Guards, 181
Brasov, 212–213, 217, 222
Bridges, 11, 35, 72, 272
Brothel, 191
Bucharest, 196, 201, 205, 208, 212
Budapest, 239, 241–242, 251, 254
Bullet train, 144, 176
Bunker, 194–195, 274
Buskers, 56

C
Cabin, 36, 64, 76, 97–98, 105, 111, 115, 127, 165, 177, 179, 181, 185, 194, 239, 277
Cable Cars, 14–15, 156–157, 170–171, 221
Cacophony, 107
Cairo Lancy, 298
Cakes, 250, 266
Camels, 117–118
Canals, 71, 84, 90, 94–95, 186
Carpathians, 217
Carriage Attendants, 64
Castles: Bran, Schonbrunn, Steen, 7, 212–213, 255
Cathedrals: Antwerp, Cologne, Lund, Moscow, Warsaw, 10–11, 15, 44, 66, 74–75, 86–87, 92, 256, 259, 277–278, 288
Cemetery: Moscow, Sighisaora, Warsaw, 197–198, 234–235
Changing of the Guards, 57, 78, 93

Charles Bridge, 270–271
Cherries, 161
China, 97, 124–125, 129, 136–137, 145, 150, 153–154, 165, 174, 177, 179, 201, 210, 262
Chita, 97, 180
Choyr, 119
Christine, xii, 243
Churches: Moscow, St. Petersburg, Vienna, Warsaw, 5, 11, 33, 44, 50, 56, 66–67, 86, 92, 206, 232–233, 236, 246, 251, 255, 258–259, 266, 269
Cloisonne, 159
Coffee and John, 177
Collette, 60–61, 63, 75, 77, 81, 90
Cologne, 10–11, 46, 57, 275, 277, 282, 285
Copenhagen, 16–20, 26, 45
Courtyard House, 129, 131
Craft shop, 266
Czech Republic, 260–261, 280

D
Danil, 77, 96
Danish party, 16–17
David L, 27, 59
Decembrists, 189
Denmark, 16, 21, 25, 27, 45, 47
Dog Team, 32
Dracula, 212
Dragon Boat, 160

E
Eau de Cologne, 282
Emperor, 133–134, 136–137, 140, 145, 160
England, 57, 106, 141, 165, 222, 243, 294

Erlian, 123
Eurostar, 2, 283, 286
Eurovision, 59
Executive Car, 2
Eye Patch man, 154

F
Family, 34, 36, 38–39, 59, 68, 73, 83, 96, 103–104, 134, 138, 160, 165, 183, 224, 265
Ferris Wheel, 256
Firsts, 18
Football, 121, 283
Forbidden City, 131–133, 155, 160, 177
Forests, 99, 187
Fountain, 6, 9, 79–80, 88, 93
Four Bridges, 72
Friends, 10, 19, 47, 59, 81, 152, 201, 210, 249, 298

G
Germany, 10–11, 47–48, 251, 261, 276–277, 283
Giant, 3, 6–7, 56
Gill, 19, 24–25, 30–33, 46, 53, 211
Gina, 241, 243, 249, 257, 260
Globe Theatre, 297
Gobi Desert, 118, 122
Goods Trains, 97, 101, 108, 187, 199
Gorky, 100
Gothenburg, 26–27, 42
Graffiti, 203, 253
Great Wall, 125, 140, 156
Guides, 147, 257

H
Hail, 194
Hangzhou, 167, 174

Hapsburgs, 255, 268
Hard Rock Cafe, 201, 211, 247, 261, 274, 297–298
Harrods, 293
Hawkers, 106, 129, 143
Helen, 47, 57
Hermitage, 65, 68
Heroes Square, 247
Hop-on Hop-off, 21
Horses, 22, 88, 117, 145, 251
Hot Chocolate, 106, 207, 258
Hotels, 196, 251, 297
Houses of Parliament, 290
Huang Shan, 167, 169–170, 174, 177
Hungary, 238, 241–243, 248
Husky Puppies, 31–32
Hutongs, 131, 149

I
Ice Creams, 50, 79
Ice Hotel, 30, 34–35
Idiots Cafe, 74
Industry, 35, 42
Irkutsk, 186

J
Jan Kipura, 46
Jan Palach, 263
Japanese Tourists, 199, 221
Jewish Cemetery, 53, 276
Jo, 83, 90–91, 96–97, 101, 104–107, 110, 118, 120–121, 123–124, 132, 137–138, 140–141, 143–144, 147–150, 153, 156, 163, 179, 186–187, 190–191
Joke, 78, 101, 233–234

K
Karen, 251
Karlstad, 38, 41
Kate, 60–61, 75, 81
Kiruna, 26, 28, 33, 35
Krasnaya Strela, 63, 97

L
Lenin, 65, 78, 88, 92
Lime Street, 2, 298
Linda, 261, 285–287, 293
Lions, 135, 155
Little Mermaid, 22
Liverpool, 26, 121, 202, 298
Liz, 261
Lorelei, 11
Lost in translation, 186
Love Locks, 84
Luggage, 2, 10, 16, 19, 25, 28, 35–36, 40, 42, 47, 57, 59–60, 63, 76, 81, 96, 163, 174, 177, 196–197, 213, 223, 242–243, 275, 283, 286

M
Malmo, 26–27, 42, 44
Marie Curie, 48, 57
Market Stalls, 192, 266
Metro Stations, 63, 177, 199
Michael, 133, 136, 138–139, 155, 177
Ming Tombs, 143
Mongolia, 97, 109, 112–113, 118, 124, 127
Moscow, 57, 59–61, 63, 76, 81, 83–84, 86, 90–91, 95–97, 99–100, 106–107, 163–165, 176–177, 179, 182, 191–193, 196–197, 199, 203, 205, 210–211, 221, 235, 274
Moscow Bath House, 81

Motorbike, 117, 152, 159, 177
Mum, 224, 243, 265, 298
Museums, 11, 35, 48, 113, 209, 213, 220

N
New Brighton, 189
Nicholas, 49, 65, 92, 97, 103
Nizhny Novograd, 100
Nonnberg Abbey, 258
Noodles, 102, 106, 122, 190
Novodevichy Cemetery, 197
Nuclear Bunker, 274

O
Ob, 105
Old Arbat, 202
Om, 105
Opera House, 250, 253
Oresund bridge, 25, 45

P
Palace, 38, 56, 65, 68, 73, 86–87, 92, 133–134, 160, 175, 208, 251, 253, 255, 259, 290, 295
Panda, 52, 56–57
Panic attacks, 96, 147
Paula, 2
Peacock Clock, 70
Penny, 1–2, 6, 10, 138, 286
Perm, 101
Peter and Paul Fortress, 74
Pipe Band, 28
Poland, 47–48, 57
Ponchos, 193
Poseidon, 27
Prague, 260–261, 269
Pyjamas, 104, 113, 152

Q
Qing Dynasty, 133
Quiet Reflections, 59, 149

R
Rain, 74–75, 152, 189, 193–194, 222, 238
Ravens, 295–296
Red Arrow, 63, 76
Red Square, 60, 62, 78, 80, 83, 91, 192
Reflections, 20, 38, 254
Reserved Seats, 212
Rickshaws, 152
Rivers, 14, 108, 168
Rock Ferry, 14, 59
Romania, 196–197, 205, 208, 210, 234, 237, 239, 266
Romanovs, 74
Rubens Paintings, 5
Russia, 33, 57, 59–61, 65, 74, 76, 78, 80, 86, 91, 96–97, 99–100, 112, 118, 124, 205
RYM Department Store, 79, 91

S
Salzburg, 256
Samovar, 100, 127
Sandra, 47, 57
Schonbrunn, 251, 255
Shanghai, 164–165, 167, 174–175
Shunting Engines, 125, 182
Siberia, 80, 109, 127, 180, 186, 189–190
Sighisaora, 222, 225, 229
Silk Museum, 141
Silver tray, 158
Simon, 1, 4, 6, 138, 150, 286
Singing, 8, 39, 139, 201, 232, 259, 264

Skansen, 35–36, 41, 211
Small Holdings, 117
Sniffer Dog, 181
Snow, 28, 30–31, 33, 37, 180, 261
Souvenirs, 127, 192
Sparrows, 197
St. Petersburg, 61, 63, 65, 92, 97, 189
Statues, 90, 93, 135, 145, 196, 198–199, 201, 209, 244, 248, 254, 271
Stockholm, 28, 35–36, 211
Summer Palace, 73, 160
Sunsets, 189
Sweden, 19, 25–26, 33, 35, 41–42, 47, 53
Symphony, 99, 107

T
Tadeuz, 57
Tangkou, 169, 177
Tanks, 150
Taxi Drivers, 48, 129–130, 145, 147, 153, 155–156, 260, 287
Tea Ceremony, 131, 136, 155, 160
Terezin Camp, 275–276
Terracotta Warriors, 145
Thai girl, 16
Thames River, 294–296
Tiananmen Square, 149, 154
Tinctures, 71
Tivoli Gardens, 45
Toboggan Run, 157
Tower of London, 293, 295
Tracy, 139, 156–157, 160, 177
Traitors Gate, 295
TransManchurian Train, 163
TransMongolian Train, 95, 111–113

TransSiberian Train, 97
Transylvania, 212, 225, 239

U
Ukraine, 196, 205
Ulan Bataar, 97, 111–112
Ulan-Ude, 97, 111
Ultimate Tour, 270
Underground Tour, 269

V
Vannen Lake, 42
Vices of Adults Sculpture, 95
Vicky, 90, 96, 149, 153–157, 159, 161, 163–164, 168–169, 173, 175, 177, 179, 183, 186–187, 190–192, 194, 196, 199, 205–207, 210, 212, 221, 224, 227–228, 233, 235, 237, 239, 241, 243
Vienna, 241, 250–251, 254, 260
Viktor Tsoi, 203
Violin, 243
Visas, 115, 181
Vivienne, 148, 177
Vlad Tepes, 212, 217, 225
Vladimir, 99
Vodka, 277

W
Walking Tours, 78, 133, 269, 274
Warsaw, 46–48, 57, 59
Wencelas Square, 261, 263
West Kirby, 189
Westminster, 286, 288, 290, 296
Wheel changing, 112
White Tower, 294, 296
Wild Horses, 117
Winter Palace, 65, 68, 73
Wirral, 189, 261

Wolves?, 239
Wonder Woman, 24
World Cup Match, 283

X
Xi'an, 144–145, 177

Y
Yannu 1905 District Sculpture, 76
Yaroslavsky Station, 96
Yellow Mountains and Peak names, 163, 171
Ykaterinburg, 103, 190
Ystad, 44
Yurts, 116, 118

Z
Zen, 301
Zhukov, 89
Zoo, 4, 15, 251